About Island Press

Island Press is the only nonprofit organization in the United States whose principal purpose is the publication of books on environmental issues and natural resource management. We provide solutions-oriented information to professionals, public officials, business and community leaders, and concerned citizens who are shaping responses to environmental problems.

In 2005, Island Press celebrates its twenty-first anniversary as the leading provider of timely and practical books that take a multidisciplinary approach to critical environmental concerns. Our growing list of titles reflects our commitment to bringing the best of an expanding body of literature to the environmental community throughout North America and the world.

Support for Island Press is provided by the Agua Fund, The Geraldine R. Dodge Foundation, Doris Duke Charitable Foundation, Ford Foundation, The George Gund Foundation, The William and Flora Hewlett Foundation, Kendeda Sustainability Fund of the Tides Foundation, The Henry Luce Foundation, The John D. and Catherine T. MacArthur Foundation, The Andrew W. Mellon Foundation, The Curtis and Edith Munson Foundation, The New-Land Foundation, The New York Community Trust, Oak Foundation, The Overbrook Foundation, The David and Lucile Packard Foundation, The Winslow Foundation, and other generous donors.

The opinions expressed in this book are those of the author(s) and do not necessarily reflect the views of these foundations.

Skinny Streets and
Green Neighborhoods

Skinny
Streets

and

Green

Neighborhoods

Design for Environment and Community

Cynthia Girling

Ronald Kellett

ISLANDPRESS

Washington • Covelo • London

Library of Congress Cataloging-in-Publication data.

Girling, Cynthia L., 1952–

Skinny streets and green neighborhoods : design for environment and community / Cynthia Girling, Ronald Kellett.

p.   cm.

Includes bibliographical references and index.

ISBN 1-59726-028-2 (cloth : alk. paper) — ISBN 1-55963-337-9 (pbk. : alk. paper)

1. City planning—United States.   2. Neighborhood planning—United States.   3. Greenways—United States.   4. Sustainable architecture—United States.   5. Sustainable buildings—United States—Design and construction.   6. United States—Environmental conditions. I. Kellett, Ronald.   II. Title.

HT167.G57 2005

307.1′216′0973—dc22   2005013821

British Cataloguing-in-Publication data available.

Printed on recycled, acid-free paper ♾

Design by Paul Hotvedt

Manufactured in the United States of America

10 9 8 7 6 5 4 3 2 1

For Cameron

Contents

Preface

The environmental dimensions of "city making" have figured
prominently among the concerns and priorities of more than a
generation of planners, landscape architects, architects, designers,
and builders whose work has guided the growth and renewal of
modern cities. The work of Rachel Carson, Paul Ehrlich, the
Club of Rome, and others in scientific disciplines warned that
attributes of where and how we live will eventually overload the
limits of land, air, and water resources necessary to sustain life.[1]
Ian McHarg outlined a method to act on that warning by planning for cities in collaboration with nature, and Victor Olgyay
linked the form and organization of cities, city blocks, and buildings to climate and to opportunities to heat, cool, and light buildings naturally.[2] The oil embargo and ensuing energy crisis of 1973
and 1974 elevated awareness of the implications of urban form,
block orientation, and building design for transportation, space
conditioning, and demand for fossil fuels. Michael Hough and
Anne Spirn, and more recently many others, have challenged us
to work beyond mitigation of environmental impact to shape urban form and functions around more artful and technically sophisticated partnerships with nature and natural functions.[3] Even
more recently, the work of William Morrish, Patrick Condon,
and others has connected these priorities to planning and design
at the scale of neighborhoods, the ubiquitous, everyday landscape
of contemporary city making and urban design.[4]

How far have we come and what have we learned? Village
Homes, in Davis, California, a benchmark of "green neighborhoods," is thirty-something. Seaside, Florida, a benchmark of the
"new urbanism" and of compact, mixed-use development, is
twenty-something. How much better are we now at shaping urban development patterns with sensitivity to land, air, water, and
people? At integrating natural with urban form? At integrating
urban with environmental functions? At making all part of the
everyday business of development?

Such questions bring us to this book, *Skinny Streets and Green
Neighborhoods.* We, the authors, are teachers and researchers based
in the disciplines of architecture and landscape architecture. Our

work and teaching are about place making at the scale of neighborhoods—the most prevalent scale and most ubiquitous form of urbanization. At this scale, we are particularly focused on the role, and the opportunity, of environment—land, air, water, and urban forest—for the forms and patterns of development. We are drawn to this scale and focus for several reasons. Chief among them is the opportunity to make tangible, positive contributions to the experience of the everyday built environment that most of us share daily. Although a humble and everyday place, the contemporary neighborhood development is also a deceptively complex urban design problem.

Neighborhoods represent a typical increment of urban development, a common but significant building block of contemporary cities, which is situated at a fascinating intersection of issues, scales, and expertise. Neighborhoods are large enough in scale to beg questions (and opportunities) of systems and network planning, yet small enough in scale and built from sufficiently small parts to require design. Issues of design and the relationship of well-designed parts to well-planned wholes are both visible and manageable.

New neighborhoods commonly form where the natural systems of environment and landscape meet human priorities of land use and transportation. They form where the spatial priorities of urban design and architecture meet the engineering and economic priorities of public works and real estate. Thus they challenge us to think and work across scales (from regions to rooms), across disciplines (from environmental science to economics), across professional domains (from planning to real estate development), and with many different people of very different agendas (from politicians and developers to homeowners).

Although we are interested in neighborhoods of many sizes and kinds—new, old, greenfield, grayfield, brownfield, infill—we and other professionals are most frequently called upon to inform the planning and design of new suburban neighborhoods. By even the most conservative estimates, suburban neighborhoods have been and remain (at least statistically) the major urban construction project of the past century in the United States. Yet this ubiquitous, everyday built environment benefits relatively little from rigorous planning or evaluation. Without such guidance, the accumulated built results often default to a weakly formed matrix of land uses, banal buildings, and automobile-dominated transportation networks and parking lots that do not serve people well and that detract from the quality of the built and natural environment. We can and should do better.

Our attempt here to contribute to something "better" centers on increasing understanding of the physical forms and patterns of neighborhoods and the impact they hold for the character and quality of life, place, and community. We seek to sharpen awareness of the environmental implications (and opportunities) for land, air, water, and habitat within these patterns. Because we also care deeply for the quality and vitality of civic and economic life, we consider environment not only as a context but also a partner, one among many forces shaping the planning and design of vital neighborhoods.

Our focus on the scale of a neighborhood is not meant to imply that environmental quality at other scales is unimportant or ineffective. Clearly, environmental opportunities also exist for energy conservation, material resource efficiency, and indoor air quality primarily at the scale of buildings. Additional opportunities for land, air, and water quality occur at the scale of regional land use and transportation patterns. However, the neighborhood is where people live; it is the environment most widely shared and most likely to be positively influenced by the decisions and actions of everyday people.

While others have tackled many of the land use, transportation, and urban design dimensions of neighborhood scale development, we are more interested here in environment—specifically, in how good urban design and good environmental design might collaborate. That said, this book is about the physical forms and patterns of cities that must work in partnership with nature. It is about integrating environmental form and functions with urban form and functions. It is as much about the patterns of land use, open space, and streets that shape our neighborhoods as it is about the quality of land, air, and water and of urban forests and the implications and opportunities each holds for the quality and vitality of neighborhoods.

When well informed and strategically applied, planning and design factor significantly into successfully integrating environmental and urban forms and functions. "Greener" alternatives, in particular, depend on cultivating the methods of thinking that "see" the patterns of environment and urban form together as a "whole." This books provides crucial access to creative examples that celebrate the connections between the two.

Development patterns of comparable density, land uses, and pedestrian connectivity, for example, can either compete with or complement other dimensions of environmental performance. Dense, mixed-use patterns of fine-grained street networks have many positive attributes, such as better distribution and proximity of services, better connectivity for vehicles and pedestrians, greater street tree opportunities, and—potentially at least—less vehicle use and fewer vehicle miles traveled. These same development patterns, however, may also compromise environmental performance in such areas as urban forest preservation, impervious surface area, and stormwater runoff. Their extensive networks of streets increase impervious surface area and tend to increase runoff. This in turn increases the quantity and rate at which runoff-borne pollutants enter watersheds. At the same time, alternative development types that reduce environmental impacts are not inevitably less dense, less mixed use, or less connective. It is indeed possible to design dense, mixed-use developments that perform at least as well as lower-density alternatives on measures of tree cover, water quality, transportation management, and infrastructure cost.

Seeing environment and urban form combined as a whole is important because their physical pattern affects overall quality and performance. The most influential differences of pattern—the amount and location of land set aside for open space, the amount and location of land allocated to streets, and the design of the street and drainage networks—are embedded in the strategies of physical planning and design. However, it is possible to design better developments only if strategically situated, interdependent networks of open space, streets, utilities, and land use can be planned and designed together from the outset.

Development patterns that diminish environmental impacts can return corollary civic and economic benefits at the same time. Surface stormwater systems, for example, not only mitigate runoff and water quality impacts but also potentially offer a nearby, connective open space network, a valuable amenity. Furthermore, if streets can be reduced in size or extent or both, they will have lower impacts and can cost less.

Skinny Streets and Green Neighborhoods is about these and

other issues, ideas and principles that underlie "greener" forms and patterns of neighborhood-scale development. Our intended audience includes planners, designers, developers, elected officials, landowners, neighbors, and others who initiate, regulate, influence, or simply care about the physical planning and design of new development in their communities. We seek to expand awareness of the issues as well as access to the instructive research, best practices, and convincing examples that artfully integrate the natural environment with city making. We hope that the knowledge, examples, and confidence gained through this book can make better environmental performance more integral to expectations of and actions for development.

The Introduction and Chapter 1 frame issues and themes that are germane to a green neighborhood. We allocate a significant portion of the book to built or planned models that articulate instructive lessons for the practice of compact development in partnership with the environment. The most fully presented of these models are the eight measured whole "neighborhood" case studies presented in Chapter 2. The U.S. or Canadian neighborhoods depicted range in scale from under 100 acres to over 1,500 acres and date from 1929 to the planned-but-not-yet-built. Each neighborhood is measured and illustrated to highlight (and enable comparison of) how their physical form and pattern integrate compact development and environment. Together, these models provide a sample of best principles and practices at a variety of sizes and scales. Specific strategies of these models and several others are discussed in greater detail in the remaining chapters. Chapters 3 through 5 consider neighborhoods' constituent systems of network and fabric in shades of green (generally natural) and gray (generally built), while Chapters 6 and 7 consider the particular role of urban forest and water. Chapter 8 considers a future in which green neighborhood design, wherein urban and natural forms and processes are fully integrated as a matter of course, not exception.

Acknowledgments

Many people have contributed in varied ways to this book, and we thank them all. We particularly thank the Departments of

Architecture and Landscape Architecture and the School of Architecture and Allied Arts at the University of Oregon for supporting our work and for providing many opportunities to develop the topics represented here in our courses and design studios. A similar thank you goes to the Landscape Architecture Program, School of Architecture and Landscape Architecture, at the University of British Columbia.

The Center for Housing Innovation, the School of Architecture and Allied Arts, and the John Yeon Charitable Trust at the University of Oregon; the Canadian Embassy in Washington, D.C.; Opsis Architecture; and Island Press all provided financial support for documenting and illustrating case studies and examples.

Numerous former students and research assistants contributed directly and indirectly to the manuscript, case studies, and examples. Among them are Claire Tebbs, Talley Fisher, Rachel Guedon, Aaron Lemchen, Jay Martin, Dior Popko, Jacqueline Rochefort, Christine Roe, Allen Schmidt, and Keara Watson. We owe particular appreciation to Weston Becker for his assistance in developing the case study format.

Kenneth Helphand, Rene Kane, and our editor Jeff Hardwick all helped refine the manuscript.

Finally, but certainly not least, we thank the many planners, developers, architects, landscape architects, and community members who generously shared their time, resources, and knowledge to assist us with case studies and examples.

Introduction

> Urban form directly affects habitat, ecosystems, endangered species, and
> water quality through land consumption, habitat fragmentation and
> replacement of natural cover with impervious surfaces.
>
> U.S. Environmental Protection Agency, *Our Built and Natural
> Environments*

Urban development in the United States reached a suburban tipping point shortly after World War II. In the years immediately
following the war, about half of the country's 140 million people lived in metropolitan (urban) areas and about half lived in
nonmetropolitan (rural) areas. By 1950, the population distribution had shifted more heavily to metropolitan areas—the tipping
point had been reached, after which urban populations exceeded
rural populations. This shift accelerated with subsequent population growth in the decades that followed. By 2000, two genera-
tions later, the U.S. population had doubled to about 281 million
and the people in metropolitan areas outnumbered the nonmetropolitan population by about four to one.

Where that population tended to settle within metropolitan
areas is the more significant trend. The U.S. Census Bureau de-
fines suburban population as the population in a metropolitan
area minus the population of the central city. The preponderance
of metropolitan area growth of the past fifty years was concentrated in the suburbs (50 percent), while central city population
(30.3 percent) declined. By 2000, suburbs had become home for
roughly half the U.S. population.[1]

While the population roughly doubled between 1940 and
2000, the housing stock tripled. In 1940, there were just over 37
million housing units in the United States. Over the next sixty
years, population slightly more than doubled (214 percent) while
average household size shrank by about a third (30 percent, from
3.68 to 2.59 persons).[2] The combination of increasing population and decreasing household size significantly accelerated demand for new housing units. By 2000, the U.S. housing stock had
expanded to about 116 million units.

Due in part to a convergence of multiple social, economic,

and policy factors, by 2000 home ownership rates had increased from about 55 percent to 67.4 percent despite the fact that the overall number of households competing for homeownership increased at the same time.[3] The majority of the new households formed could afford to buy housing units, and many chose to make that investment in larger, single-family, detached houses outside central cities. The urban development patterns of these new places also changed. Between 1950 and 2000, for example, the typical new home in the United States more than doubled in floor area, from two bedrooms and one bath in 1,000 square feet or less (at an average cost of $11,000) to three or more bedrooms and two and a half baths in 2,265 square feet plus garage (at an average cost of $206,400).[4]

These new houses were built in more decentralized and distributed suburban models rather than the compact urban models common in pre–World War II cities. This in turn precipitated a substantial investment in automobiles and transportation infrastructure (roads and parking lots) needed to connect widely distributed homes with work and services. Concurrently, the urban areas and the neighborhoods in which these houses were situated also changed significantly. Cities became much less compact, and land uses became less mixed and more stratified overall. Urban areas grew both in number and in area. The urbanized land area of the largest metropolitan areas of the United States, for example, quadrupled between 1954 and 2000.[5]

With some regional variation, the rate at which nonurban land has been developed has greatly outpaced the rate at which population has been growing—by roughly two to one. From 1950 to 1970, for example, the population of Phoenix grew 300 percent while its urbanized area grew 630 percent to become one of the more telling illustrations of poorly managed growth. Much of the outward urban expansion in Phoenix was due to very-low-density suburban development. From 1970 to 1990, the population of Nashville grew 28 percent while its urban area expanded 41 percent, and the population of Charlotte grew 63 percent while its urbanized area expanded 129 percent. Other cities lost population while concurrently growing outward in size. Detroit, for example, shrank 7 percent in population while its urbanized area expanded 28 percent. The population of Pittsburgh shrank 9 percent while its urbanized area expanded 30 percent.

While population growth and urban land area are coarse indicators of the implications of development pattern, other evidence illustrates how cities often decentralize within their own borders. Many larger U.S. cities (particularly those in warm, dry climates in the West and the South) grew during the 1990s, about a quarter of them at rates greater than 16 percent. Many also attracted new population to their central areas. However, in most cases, with some regional variation, central city population growth was balanced by losses in the neighborhoods immediately surrounding central areas and overwhelmed by much higher rates of growth near suburban edges. Overall, the populations of most U.S. cities decentralized toward suburban perimeters during the 1990s. The Southeast, for example, set the pace with a suburban growth rate three times that of central cities in the region.[6]

These trends show little indication of slowing down. On the contrary, they seem to be increasing. Between 1992 and 1997, the national rate of urbanization more than doubled, to 3 million acres annually. An urbanized footprint roughly equal to that of San Diego, California, was added over the five years.[7]

Even cities noted for their vital centers and compact growth share this experience. Vancouver, British Columbia, for example, is widely cited for its dense, livable central city and robust investment in urban infill. Between 2002 and 2003—a very strong year for residential construction and sales in the central city—that population remained unchanged while population outside the central city increased by just over 1 percent. In other words, despite significant new dwelling construction in a thriving central city, Vancouver was unable to redirect net growth away from all but a few of its suburbs.[8]

This pace and extent of suburban growth has significant consequences, including its now-familiar environmental impacts. Natural features are removed to make way for development— wooded areas are cleared, streams are culverted or channeled, wetlands are filled or fenced, and topography is leveled. Agricultural land, natural resource lands (forests and wetlands, for example), and habitat areas have been forever lost, or new development has cut them into smaller, less-productive fragments, with significant environmental and economic consequences. Dispersed land uses also affect livability. Shopping, recreation, and schools are located far away from one another and often separated from residential areas by wide, fast streets and expansive parking lots. Travel distances increase while pedestrian safety decreases, making it difficult to live without automobiles.

Typical suburban development patterns feature poorly connected street networks. These networks in turn influence people's travel choices and behavior. Commonly, only one route may exist from place to place, and it is often "the long way" as the crow flies. Sized and scaled for moving vehicles, the travel lanes of the network's streets precipitate poor transit ridership and service. Pedestrian and bicycle facilities are second class and dangerous. Sidewalks are often adjacent to travel lanes (with no planting strips), thus exposing pedestrians directly to rapidly moving traffic vehicles. Residential streets often do not have sidewalks; the sidewalks of those that do are interrupted by driveways and thus dominated by cars and garages. As people are forced to drive more, fossil fuel consumption increases. This increase in turn affects air quality, which continues to decline despite significant improvements in the design and engineering of cars and fuels. The bigger symptom of all this driving is the increase in greenhouse gases and in the rate of global warming.

Water resources and the quality of water near urban areas have also declined. Typical suburban development dramatically increases the area of impervious surfaces, such as pavement and roofs. Much of the surfaces that are not impervious consists of chemically managed lawns or landscape that, together with greater concentrations of automobiles, contributes to erosion, pollution, and reduced ground water.

Other, less tangible environmental and health consequences of sprawl have been more difficult to establish. However, as the science, technology, and tools to measure these consequences have become more sophisticated, the adverse effects of sprawl on our health and quality of life have been documented. For example, many suburban dwellers spend much of their lives in cars; as distances and congestion increase, so does commuting time. As a result, overall human health has declined, as indicated by increased rates of obesity, heart disease, diabetes, and respiratory illness.[9]

Nonetheless, suburbs remain the destination of choice for most people. And by almost any demographic or economic measure, building this ever-expanding suburban landscape remains the dominant planning and design project of our day. Ellen Dunham-Jones concludes that approximately 76 percent of new population growth, 95 percent of new office space (and jobs), and 75 percent of new construction expenditures are concentrated in the suburbs.[10] Although suburban growth has persisted in many cities, the development patterns into which it has been accommodated have begun to change. The contemporary challenge for many cities is how to stem the rate of outward expansion by encouraging so-called smart growth—more compact, pedestrian-friendly development patterns that consume less land and allow transportation choices beyond the automobile.

Growing Compact

Portland, Oregon, is one example of a city that has, since the mid-1990s, focused on directing population growth into targeted compact neighborhoods. Working within the context of state growth management policies that require new development to be within urban growth boundaries, the metropolitan region coordinated overall growth and land use and transportation planning in its Region 2040 plan. According to this plan, growth would be concentrated at town centers located at transportation nodes, most along light rail lines. Orenco Station illustrates one successful town center (see the case study in Chapter 2).

Orenco Station is a new "greenfield," transit-oriented neighborhood in Hillsboro, Oregon, on the western perimeter of the Portland metropolitan area, approximately 20 miles from downtown (Figure 0.1). Located at a rapid transit station, Orenco was planned in 1995 and 1996 to accommodate 1,835 dwellings and a mixed commercial center on a 156-acre site (Figure 0.2). Density targets were set at a gross density of twelve dwellings per acre—roughly three times that of the prevailing pattern in Hillsboro and other Portland suburbs. As of 2004, the development was achieving those targets (Figure 0.3).

Orenco Station demonstrates how transit-oriented, compact development patterns can succeed in a perimeter suburb and shows that planning and design quality is crucial to that success. Initial sales exceeded projections, and dwelling unit prices ran

Figure 0.1 Orenco Station relative to Portland, Oregon.

Figure 0.2 Orenco Station plan in context.

Figure 0.3 Orenco Station shortly after start of construction.

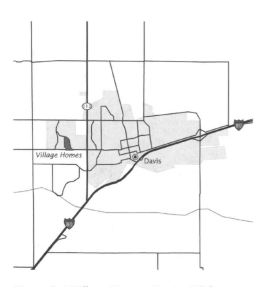

Figure 0.4 Village Homes, Davis, California.

about 20 to 30 percent above area averages. The development's appeal has been attributed in part to its physical planning and design—the social vitality of a mixed-use town center and community open space in combination with the pedestrian orientation and scale of the streets.[11]

A subsequent evaluation of social and transportation indicators reported a strong sense of community and some improvement in transit use as well. A convincing majority, 78 percent, of the residents surveyed reported a greater sense of community compared to their previous neighborhoods. Almost three-quarters of residents reported an increase in transit use over their previous neighborhoods, but they still use private automobiles for three-quarters of their commuting trips.[12] With triple the residential density of its neighbors, Orenco Station illustrates some successful strategies for land conservation and air pollution reductions. Its weaknesses are that issues of water quality, urban forest, and habitat have not been planning or design priorities.

Growing Green

Village Homes, near Davis, California, is widely considered a prototype green neighborhood (Figure 0.4). Conceived, designed, and developed by Michael and Judy Corbett in the mid-1970s as an adaptation of Stein and Wright's 1929 plan for Radburn, America's first model garden city, Village Homes demonstrates a small-scale neighborhood plan woven together with open spaces to achieve goals of community, energy conservation, and environmental awareness. In addition, the development demonstrates many socially, ecologically, and economically innovative features, including a pedestrians-first, automobiles-second circulation network, surface drainage systems, neighborhood orchards and gardens, and lots and buildings orientated for solar energy (Figure 0.5).

Approximately a third of the development's site plan is allocated to community and public open space. Another 18 percent is reserved for public streets. At the core of the plan is a hierarchical network of open spaces. Beginning at the smallest scale, private courtyards and gardens adjacent to houses connect to small common areas between small groups of houses. These in turn connect to larger greenways that accommodate stormwater drainage and pedestrian and bicycle paths at the scale of a block. The greenways connect to larger public open spaces and agricultural landscapes of orchards, vineyards, and community gardens.

A connected network of pedestrian and bicycle routes is well integrated with the open space and the street network, making it easier to walk or bike from one part of Village Homes to another than it is to drive. The longest travel distance within the network is less than five minutes, and many routes can be negotiated without crossing a street. Elements of automobile transportation are secondary and much less direct. The entire street network is served by only one street, which lies along the east side of the plan. All local streets leading from it are very narrow, curving, service-oriented cul-de-sacs.

Open space and low-density residential land uses dominate the Village Homes plan (Figure 0.6). One liability is the lack of commercial services nearby. A small commercial area includes a restaurant and offices; however, most shopping and other daily services are within biking (not walking) distance. As a result, most residents drive to commercial centers in Davis, Woodland, or Sacramento for more significant purchases.

The stormwater management and food production capacity enabled by the open space network of Village Homes is significant. Within the open space network is a finely scaled open-drainage system (Figure 0.7). With the exception of peak storm events, the open spaces manage all of the stormwater runoff generated on-site at lower capital and infrastructure maintenance costs than those experienced in adjacent neighborhoods. In addition, residents are able to grow about 24 percent of their own fruits and vegetables (about a third more than adjacent neighborhoods) and gain modest income from an almond crop.[13]

This green neighborhood works and is highly valued by the residents. Surveys of Village Homes and adjacent neighborhoods reveal that Village Homes residents know more than twice as many of their neighbors. And like Orenco Station, the strong sense of community has economic value. When Village Homes houses are put up for sale, they tend to sell quickly and at a premium compared to similar houses in adjacent neighborhoods.[14]

Despite the considerable contribution of Village Homes to environmentally oriented development patterns, it also has

Figure 0.5 Village Homes plan in context.

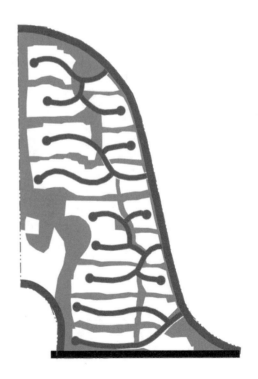

Figure 0.6 Village Homes: green and gray networks.

Figure 0.7 Village Homes: drainage within an open space corridor.

environmental liabilities—notably its size and density (75 acres and 240 dwellings, or 3.5 per gross acre—a density roughly equal to the more conventionally patterned suburban neighborhoods adjacent). Neighborhood-scale development patterns of that size and density generally conserve land poorly and fail to generate sufficient market for the transit and on-site services, or the interneighborhood connectivity that tends to reduce demand for automobile trips.

On the other hand, Village Homes has attracted residents interested in reducing environmental impact through other, more behaviorally based means. Compared to adjacent neighborhoods, Village Homes residents tend to own fewer cars and to use them less, generating approximately 16 percent fewer vehicle miles per car. They also consume about 34 percent less electricity, largely due to the passive and active use of solar energy for space conditioning and hot water heating made possible by strategic orientation of the blocks, lots, and buildings through site planning.[15]

Growing Compact *and* Green

If evaluated against an overriding goal to manage urban growth and concurrently conserve energy, quality of life, community, and land, air, and water quality, how does a model of a compact neighborhood like Orenco Station compare to a green neighborhood like Village Homes?

Although it is impossible to make a rigorous comparison with the data available, we can draw general conclusions (see Table 0.1). Orenco Station is certainly the better performer against measures related to land conservation. Village Homes is certainly the better performer against measures related to water quality and probably the better performer against measures related to energy conservation. More of the land of Village Homes is set aside for open space and strategically allocated to environmental, food, transportation, and social purposes; less is allocated to vehicles. However, comparisons against measures related to automobile trip demand and air quality are not possible. Although both developments perform better than conventional suburban neighborhoods, comparable information is not available to determine which of the two more effectively reduces trip demand per household. Orenco Station is certainly more supportive of transit use, and Village Homes is probably more supportive of bicycle use. Both are supportive of pedestrians. In terms of infrastructure, Village Homes costs less to develop and maintain. Both perform well against measures of community—albeit for very different reasons—and for market value relative to other neighborhoods.

Rather than determining which pattern is better, the more important question is perhaps to what degree can the two neighborhoods' positive attributes be merged to perform better against multiple environmental objectives—land, air, water, urban forest, and habitat—at the same time? Or, in physical pattern terms, how and to what degree can development patterns such as Orenco Station's be integrated with open space patterns such as Village Homes?

In the end, if current sprawling development patterns persist, the environmental consequences will be unsustainable, even devastating. More agricultural land will be consumed by sprawl, habitat will be fragmented and destroyed, pollution will increase,

Table 0.1. Key indicators comparison of Village Homes
and Orenco Statioin

	Village Homes Davis, California (established in 1975)	*Orenco Station Hillsboro, Oregon (established in 2000)*
Study area (in acres)	63.5	218.4
Land allocated to public open space (in acres)	21	20.8
% of study area	33%	10%
Land allocated to streets (in acres)	12.2	60.4
% of study area	19%	28%
Land allocated to residential uses (in acres)	26.7	88.4
% of study area	42%	40%
Dwellings	240	1,906
Net density (dwellings per acre of residential land)	9.0	21.6
Gross density (dwellings per acre of study area)	3.8	8.7

and water systems will be degraded. People will spend more and more time in traffic, while getting less and less healthy. These trajectories are well established, but solutions have been elusive. Regions, cities, and neighborhoods must find solutions to reverse these trends. Many cities have started this quest. Throughout North America, examples of nascent solutions to many of these ills can be found, but few of them tackle compact, green development holistically. We propose that green neighborhoods, as described in the chapters that follow, are the building blocks for metropolitan solutions.

Chapter 1
Green Neighborhoods

Traditional building forms and settlement patterns are the product of dialogues among natural and cultural processes.

A. W. Spirn, "New Urbanism and the Environment"

Even very large cities grow in small increments. The term "neighborhood" is frequently used to describe the urban "building blocks" of complementary land uses, transportation networks, services, and amenities. These systems are typically conceived together to benefit from the identity and location afforded by being in the same "neighborhood" as well as to leverage the substantial investment of land, capital, infrastructure, and human will it takes to create them. Cliff Moughtin quotes Boyd: "A neighborhood is formed naturally from the daily occupations of people, the distance it is convenient . . . to walk . . . to daily shopping . . . and a child to walk to school. He should not have a long walk and he should not have to cross a main traffic road. The planning of a neighborhood starts from that."[1]

While "neighborhood" can be defined in diverse ways, the term is used in this book in a spatial sense of sharing common proximity and boundary. Understood this way, neighborhoods are those broadly legible, if not precisely definable, areas of cities in which people say they live, work, learn, or play. It is also the scale at which new areas of many cities are planned. Within this definition, neighborhoods may vary substantially in physical size, shape, population, density, or character. Several may link together to form a larger, interdependent group of neighborhoods. In contemporary usage, that proximity has frequently come to be defined as the distance that one can (or would be willing to) walk to services or to a transit stop (between five and ten minutes, or one-quarter to one-half mile for most people). That represents a land area of roughly 125 to 500 acres. Neighborhoods also have edges or boundaries that differentiate one from another. These edges can vary in type and character. Some may be hard and explicit (such as a wide, heavily trafficked street), whereas others may be soft and implicit (such as a contrasting land use or a

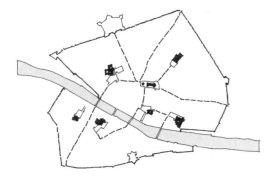

Figure 1.1 Diagrammatic neighborhood structure of Renaissance Florence. (Source: derived from Frey, *Designing the City,* p. 39)

common open space), allowing several neighborhoods to overlap or interconnect along a shared edge (Figure 1.1).

Taken together, domain and edge are the physical conditions of a neighborhood in planning and urban design. Nineteenth-century British urban theorist Ebenezer Howard and architects Raymond Unwin and Barry Parker, who gave physical form to Howard's theories, recognized the importance of these attributes of neighborhood. They shaped the Garden City, a new-town planning concept, around a "ward"—a district or quarter centered around the social institution of a school and separated from others by a greenbelt.[2] The eleven British new towns authorized by the New Towns Act of 1946—for example, Runcorn and Ipswich—are defined by the following: a ten- to fifteen-minute walking distance from the farthest home to the school; a population that supports an elementary school and local services; a clearly defined boundary (typically reinforced by landscape); a center; through traffic relegated to perimeter streets; and an architectural treatment that distinguishes it from other neighborhoods.

In the United States, Clarence Perry's 1929 essay on the neighborhood unit borrowed many themes from Howard. Perry argued that a neighborhood should be approximately 160 acres and should support a density of ten households per acre. The resulting population would support an elementary school (located at a central focal point of community services) and commercial services (located along edges with other neighborhoods). Several smaller parks and recreation areas would make up 10 percent of the land area. Neighborhood shape should be such that all households were within walking distance (less than half a mile) of a school and services. Neighborhood boundaries should follow major streets to keep high-volume traffic at the edges, reducing traffic through the neighborhood. Residential streets interior to the neighborhood could be smaller, with less automobile traffic. Only a few should connect directly to larger boundary streets.[3]

Perry's work eventually led to national neighborhood planning standards published in the industry-wide technical bulletins of the U.S. Federal Housing Administration.[4] After World War II, qualification for federal mortgage assistance was directly tied to these standards; thus they explicitly influenced the development pattern of a generation of subdivisions throughout the United States in the 1950s and 1960s.[5]

Perry's work and its antecedents have informed neighborhood planning and design practice for almost eighty years. From the planning and urban design work of Perry's contemporary Clarence Stein to the contemporary town-making principles of the Congress for the New Urbanism, planners, landscape architects, and architects have adapted and built upon his ideas and concepts (Figure 1.2). A comparison of Clarence Perry's 1929 principles of neighborhood planning with those of Duany and Plater Zyberk (1997) show extensive agreement. For both, the preferable size is a 160-acre area bounded by larger scale streets and developed at densities sufficient to support an elementary school. Exact shape is not essential but should fit within a quarter-mile (5-minute walk) circle such that all sides are roughly equidistant from the center.

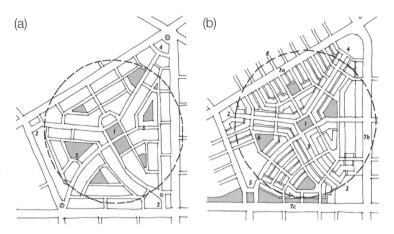

Figure 1.2 Comparison of (a) Clarence Perry's (1929) and (b) Duany and Plater-Zyberk's (1997) prototypical neighborhood plans (after *Congress for the New Urbanism,* 2000, p. 76)

1. Neighborhood institutions only at community center in the Perry version, Shops and institutions near a transit stop in the DPZ version.
2. Apartments and shopping districts at higher traffic intersections. Parking lots double as plazas in the DPZ version.
3. Narrow interior streets configured for easy access to shops and community center. A mixed use street is anchored by shopping districts in the DPZ version.
4. Civic buildings occupy prominent sites. A shopping district could substitute for a perimeter church site in the Perry version.
5. A school and related recreation spaces may be located near the edge where it can be shared with an adjacent neighborhood.
6. A playground is located in each quadrant.
7. Boulevard edges may develop with (a) the short faces of traditional blocks; (b) workshops and offices; (c) a parkway corridor.
8. Street and block patterns connect to adjacent neighborhoods to greatest extent possible.[6]

To Clarence Perry's 1929 principles of the neighborhood unit, New Urbanists such as Duany and Plater-Zyberk have added several that address the urban design and architecture of neighborhoods. Still missing are principles that address environmental factors.

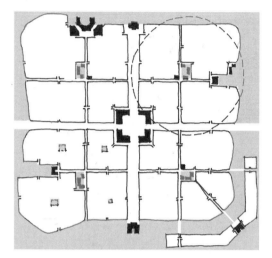

Figure 1.3 An aggregation of neighborhoods forming a village bounded by open space. (Source: derived from Duany and Plater-Zyberk, *Towns and Town-Making Principles,* 1991, p. 90)

Defining Green Neighborhoods

Many attributes embedded in the spatial models of neighborhood mentioned above offer the opportunity to improve urban environmental quality. Principles of the new urbanism, for example, generate development patterns that use land more economically than does prevailing contemporary practice. Densities are sufficiently high and land uses sufficiently mixed to increase the likelihood that daily services (stores, recreation, and schools, for example) are within walking distance. Street networks are sufficiently connective to encourage fewer automobile trips (and thus improve air quality and energy conservation) through choice of mode. Streets that make up the network are typically skinny—they are scaled and designed for equity of use among cars, bicycles, and pedestrians. Walking or bicycling becomes a viable alternative to driving for travel within the neighborhood, and transit becomes a viable option for travel outside the neighborhood.[7]

Less explicit and integral, however, are places for nature. More often, natural areas have limited or peripheral roles, typically as edges or boundaries to neighborhoods. Such roles increase the real and perceived barriers between natural and urban systems as well as weaken opportunities to integrate urban and natural functions. A more "green" model would create explicit places for nature and ecological functions, integrate them with the development pattern, and balance the competing spatial demands of open space, streets, and land uses within.

How might nature become more integral with urban development? For the sake of argument, assume that natural spaces are most often the open spaces of an urban pattern. Urban planner and observer Kevin Lynch has argued that open space is distributed in relatively few spatial patterns. In his lexicon, three patterns exist (Figure 1.4): the greenbelt (open space encloses urban development—an edge), the green wedge (open space radiates from a center), and the green network (a more broadly distributed but linked pattern of open space).[8] These patterns represent contrasting points of view about open space and, by extension, about nature in cities. In one view, open spaces tend to be large and concentrated to give size, shape, and form to the built development pattern. In the other view, open spaces tend to be smaller, more dispersed, and more selectively contiguous to increase access to and interface with the built pattern.

The linked network pattern in particular abandons the convention of giving a hard form to open space pattern and focuses instead on a more negotiated distribution and connection of diverse open space elements. Open spaces and connections could be larger, and connections to them more generous, at points of higher environmental value and lesser development value, such as near an important stream corridor. Open spaces could be smaller, and connections to them narrower, at points of high development value and lower environmental value, such as near major roads. Since this open space pattern is continuous and interconnected yet closely intertwined with urban uses at many points, nature is more easily close at hand. From many points in developed areas, people can more easily connect to the open space system and, once in the system, can move through it uninterrupted.

Clarence Stein's neighborhood prototype is an example of a networked open space pattern (Figure 1.5).[9] Stein's plan follows the convention of a school-centered service area of approximately a half-mile radius with emphasis on the amount and distribution of open space in a linear, interconnected pattern. Stein also significantly reduced land areas allocated to streets, purposefully decreased connectivity for automobiles, and increased connectivity and accessibility to commercial services for pedestrians and bicycles. This design, which fundamentally changed the development pattern from street centered to open space centered, became known as the Radburn pattern, after its best-known example in New Jersey (Figure 1.6). Despite the opportunity presented, Stein's prototype was never completed at Radburn; the small built portion did not realize potential open space connectivity at larger scales, from neighborhood to neighborhood or from neighborhood to natural areas.

More recently, architect Peter Calthorpe has made open space and resource protection a key guiding principle in his neighborhood prototype, the transit-oriented development (TOD).[10] Advocating conservation of major creeks, riparian habitat, and other environmental features, Calthorpe recommended their integration into new neighborhoods as something more than edges. This more negotiated, better integrated synthesis of open space, street network, and land use pattern presented much greater opportunity and multiple uses for natural open space beyond simple resource protection or visual amenity. Figure 1.7 illustrates Calthorpe's transformation of the original TOD

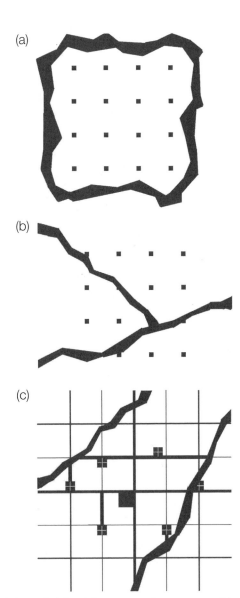

Figure 1.4 Spatial patterns of open space: (a) greenbelt, (b) green wedge, and (c) green network.

Figure 1.5 Clarence Stein's neighborhood unit. (Source: De Chiara, Panero, and Zelnik, *Time-saver Standards for Housing and Residential Development,* p. 51)

Figure 1.6 Radburn neighborhood plan. (Source: derived from Southworth and Ben-Joseph, *Streets and the Shaping of Towns and Cities,* p. 63)

concept to support a more active role for and more connective pattern of open space. Within it, opportunities were created for natural areas to serve as pedestrian and bicycle corridors that connect many kinds and scales of public space—for example, parks, schools, and town centers—as well as protect important environmental assets at the same time.

Calthorpe's diagram implies a more active relationship between the spatial patterns of open space and built development, making it a contemporary "green neighborhood" prototype. In the diagram, both natural and urban patterns are distinct and legible. Take away the built pattern, and a functional natural pattern remains; take away the natural pattern, and a functional built pattern remains. Taken together, however, a third pattern, created by the integration and interaction of the two, suggests spatial opportunities to strategically merge, layer, or juxtapose built and natural ecologies that might also be better urban places—spatially, functionally, and economically.

Achieving the potential of this emerging view of integrated open and built space presents conceptual and methodological challenges to the planning of urban development patterns. While such planning already embraces many ways to represent the patterns of built form, land use, transportation, infrastructure, and other human attributes in parallel, rarely are ecological forces and open space assets equal partners. Until built and ecological components gain equal status, opportunities to consider where they may work together or where they may compete will continue to be lost.

An Example: The Royal Avenue Plan

New neighborhoods frequently emerge at the suburban edges of cities. At these edges, emerging models of "smart growth" development patterns confront the natural resources and open spaces of rural landscapes. The most common spatial relationship between the two—open space as edge or boundary—insulates the urban from the natural, and the natural from the urban. A more closely integrated spatial relationship facilitates a more extensive and diverse palette of opportunities. Urban areas benefit from the more robust ecological functions near them, and rural landscapes benefit from better stewardship of natural resources. One example, the Royal Avenue Plan in Eugene, Oregon, provides an instructive story of the "greening" of a neighborhood-scale development pattern. The first version of the plan was shaped by land use and transportation in 1998. Over the next five years, it was reshaped to improve its ecological structure, specifically its wetland protection and natural stormwater drainage. Incrementally articulated at each iteration, the influence of these forces was ultimately reconciled in an integrated whole.

Royal Avenue (Figure 1.8) is a familiar example of an emerging growth area at the edge of a small city—in this case, a metropolitan area of about 225,000 people. Like many greenfield development sites in Oregon's Willamette Valley, this area of flat bottomland sits between the existing city limits of Eugene and an urban growth boundary immediately adjacent to valuable agricultural, timber, or natural resource land. This particular site, once annexed, is destined to form part of the western edge of Eugene and the eastern edge of a valuable wetland area.

Adjacent development is typical postwar suburban sprawl. Densities are low, and land uses are spread out and segregated. Street networks are circuitous and poorly connected. Natural features have been destroyed or urbanized—wooded areas have been cleared, streams have been culverted or channelized, wetlands have been filled or fenced, and land has been leveled. Automobiles rule. Transit service is poor, and pedestrian and bicycle facilities are few. Large expanses of impervious surfaces are connected and mechanically drained to channelized drainage ways. Most of what is not paved consists of chemically managed lawns.

In an attempt to intensify development throughout the metropolitan area, this particular 200-acre site had been designated as one of thirty-eight growth centers by a regional plan. The plan developed for this place represents a prototype of "nodal development," principles adopted to integrate growth, transportation, and environmental planning goals. The principles seek to establish a regional pattern of compact, concentrated development that favors transit- and pedestrian-oriented development.

The Royal Avenue Plan is different from many such development plans in the degree to which it reconstructs existing and historic drainage corridors and wetlands, links them in an open space network, and uses them to provide a backbone of amenities and ecological functions to serve the land uses of a new neighborhood. The site is dormant agricultural land, about 25 percent of which is converted prairie wetlands. Its proximity to a crucial

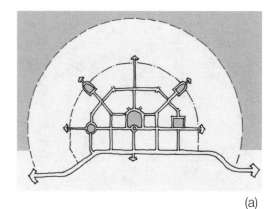

(a)

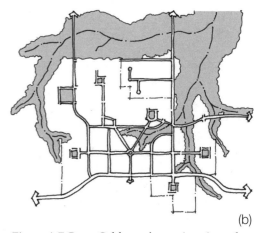

(b)

Figure 1.7 Peter Calthorpe's transit-oriented development: (a) prototype and (b) with natural resource areas. (Source: derived from Calthorpe, *The Next American Metropolis,* pp. 63 and 72)

Figure 1.8 Royal Avenue Plan in context.

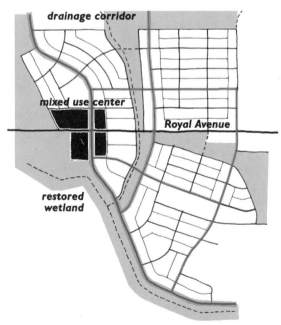

Figure 1.9 Royal Avenue Plan: green and gray networks.

regional environmental asset, an 8,000-acre wetland restoration project, precipitated a need to set aside a pair of open space corridors through the plan. These corridors serve two primary functions: to preserve the highest-quality wetlands and to drain the site and adjacent urban areas and hydrologically connect these areas with the adjacent wetlands. At the same time, the corridors also provide additional land area for wetland mitigation, passive recreation, bicycle and pedestrian routes, connections to neighborhood parks and a school, and wildlife as well as human connections to the large, adjacent natural and recreation areas (Figure 1.9).

The plan demonstrates an integration of the ecological functions of green networks and fabric and the urban functions of gray networks and fabric (Figure 1.10). It comprises three subneighborhood areas and gridded street networks modified by the open space corridors. One of these areas, a mixed-use center situated on the west side, is the commercial heart of the plan at the proposed intersection of two major streets. This commercial area is surrounded by areas of mixed uses and higher-density housing. Two other subneighborhoods, located north and south of Royal Avenue, the major east-west street, accommodate lower-density residential and related uses. A street loop connects the commercial area, parks, and school at the center of each subneighborhood. Overall net residential density will be 12 dwellings per acre, the target for all nodal developments. About 21 percent of the site is in parks and open space uses. Few automobile streets cross open space corridors, but most continue over bridges for pedestrians and bicycles (Figures 1.10 and 1.11).

Network and Fabric—Green and Gray

> Urban land as a whole will be required to assume environmental, productive and social roles in the design of cities.
>
> M. Hough, *Cities and Natural Process*

Integrating urban and ecological functions as a matter of course rather than exception depends on an understanding of how natural and urban systems coexist in cities. Our challenge is in part to cultivate the habits of mind and the methods of working that help us see the interaction of natural and urban patterns more

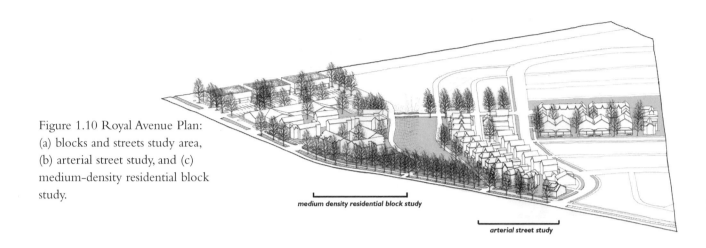

Figure 1.10 Royal Avenue Plan:
(a) blocks and streets study area,
(b) arterial street study, and (c)
medium-density residential block
study.

medium density residential block study

arterial street study

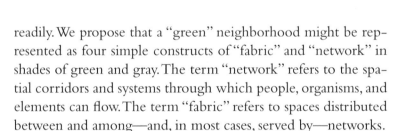

Figure 1.11 Royal Avenue Plan: arterial street with drainage and infiltration in center median.

readily. We propose that a "green" neighborhood might be represented as four simple constructs of "fabric" and "network" in shades of green and gray. The term "network" refers to the spatial corridors and systems through which people, organisms, and elements can flow. The term "fabric" refers to spaces distributed between and among—and, in most cases, served by—networks.

Green and gray modify both network and fabric and distinguish between those that serve ecological functions and those that serve primarily built, urban functions. The distinctions made are a conceptual aid to simplify the complexity and amplify the spatial implications of these important forces. In this lexicon, traditional land uses (residential, commercial, and so forth) are gray fabric, and the streets that serve them are gray networks. Public open spaces are green fabric, and the open space corridors (e.g., streams and floodways) that connect them are green networks. We use these constructs as a means of representation in the case studies presented in Chapter 2. In the remaining chapters, we define the constructs in greater depth and discuss their complex, interwoven relationships.

Figure 1.12 Royal Avenue Plan: stormwater wetland adjacent to medium-density residential block.

Chapter 2
Case Studies

Overview

If one takes the term "green neighborhood" to mean primarily residential development that integrates natural systems within its form and pattern, "green" can come in a variety of sizes and intensities. This book presents several examples, here and in other chapters (see Table 2.1, p. 24). All are U.S. or Canadian examples that, to varying degrees, integrate natural elements and systems within their development pattern. They represent a range of scales and types of neighborhood, from very small (60 acres) to very large (1,300 acres) and from very low density (fewer than one dwelling unit per gross acre) to very dense (sixty dwelling units per gross acre). Two of the examples—Radburn and Village Homes—are well known and offer useful benchmarks against which to measure the others. The remaining examples represent current practice and have been recently built or are under construction or being planned as of this writing. As a group, they present a small but instructive snapshot of contemporary, environmentally focused neighborhood-scale planning and design practice. Individually, they reveal the many ways the green and gray fabric and networks of a green neighborhood can be integrated.

To aid comparison, a common lexicon of themes, measures, graphic conventions, and formats illustrates each case, allowing comparison of significant similarities and differences among the cases. Because the cases vary significantly in size and shape, they are presented at two different scales: the larger scale is double the smaller. A common graphic scale showing a quarter-mile, or roughly five-minute walk, accompanies each case. A study area boundary for each case is delineated by a red dashed line in the illustrative plan diagrams and by a thin solid red line in the thematic plan diagrams. This boundary represents the extent of measured area. Total area reported for each case, represents all land within this boundary. In some cases, differences between published areas and those presented here may be attributed to the extent of the study area considered.

All land within the study area of a case has been assigned a use. Each land use has been graphically coded using familiar designations and colors. Because definitions of the land use designations depicted by these colors vary widely across jurisdictions, these categories have been standardized for easier comparison. The arrangement of these land uses in a case has been illustrated by superimposing a transparently colored land use on the most recent aerial photograph available. A land use bar scale immediately below the illustrative plan scales the percentage of the study area allocated to each land use. Total length of the bar represents 100 percent of the land use–colored area. Line segments allocated to each land use are scaled to illustrate their proportion of the total study area. Numeric values associated with these land uses have been rounded and their sum may not equal 100 percent.

Four thematic plan diagrams further break down the illustrative plan to highlight green and gray fabric and networks—the four principal spatial themes used in this book. In the color cases, a histogram illustrates a quantitative summary of the plan diagram. Again, associated numeric values have been rounded and their sum may not equal 100 percent. Two densities have been calculated for each case: *gross density* reports the residential intensity of the entire study area (the total number or estimate of dwelling units divided by the entire study area), and *net density* reports the residential intensity of that part of the plan allocated to housing (the total or estimated number of dwelling units divided by land area allocated to residential uses). Where known, actual dwelling counts are used; where estimated, the midpoint value in each residential land use designation is used. Finally, an image gallery of photographs, sketches, and diagrams presented by land use category illustrates the character, look, and feel of the land uses that make up the case.

Land Use Designations

The following land use designations and definitions have been used to analyze the case studies.

Open Space

Open space uses are public lands designated by the degree of disturbance and maintenance associated with them.

- *Natural areas.* Low-disturbance and low-maintenance areas (e.g., forest preserves and wetlands) that have value as environmental assets and can support only limited recreational and movement functions.
- *Parks.* Higher-disturbance and higher-maintenance areas (e.g., parks, greenways, and golf courses) that are able to support more active recreational and social functions.

Streets

Street uses are designated by right-of-way width and associated traffic load.

- *Arterial streets.* Largest-scale, highest-traffic-volume, limited-access streets designed for vehicular mobility. These have been normalized here for illustration and measurement at 90- and 75-foot rights-of-way.
- *Collector streets.* Streets intermediate in scale, traffic volume, and access that are used to gather local street traffic and connect it to local services and to arterials. Frequently used for transit. Normalized here at a 60-foot right-of-way.
- *Local streets.* Smaller-scale, low-traffic-volume streets used primarily for access to fronting properties. Normalized here at a 45-foot right-of-way.
- *Alleys.* Smallest-scale, very-low-traffic streets for secondary and service access to properties fronting a local, collector, or arterial street. Normalized here at a 20-foot right-of-way.
- *Pedestrian paths.* Dedicated pedestrian rights-of-way. Normalized here at a 7-foot right-of-way.

Residential

Residential uses are designated by the building and lot design types associated with their densities.

- *Stacked dwellings.* Dwelling types that require stacking to achieve typical net densities greater than twenty-four dwellings per acre (1,850-square-foot lot/dwelling). Typical examples include stacked or clustered townhouses and apartments sited on larger parcels with shared street access, on-site parking, yards, and entries.
- *Attached dwellings.* Dwelling types that require side-to-side or front-to-back attachment to achieve typical net densities

greater than fourteen and fewer than than twenty-three dwellings per acre (1,890- to 3,100-square-foot lot/dwelling). Typical examples include duplexes and row houses sited on smaller, individually owned parcels with private street access, on-site parking, yards, and entries.

- *Detached dwellings.* Freestanding dwelling types that achieve typical net densities up to thirteen dwellings per acre (3,350-square-foot lot/dwelling). Typical examples include a wide range of single-family, detached types sited on fee simple parcels with private street access, on-site parking, yards, and entries.

Mixed Use

Mixed-use areas are designated by the degree and character of land use mix within them.

- *Residential mixed use.* Primarily residential area with up to 25 percent compatible (typically commercial and civic) uses.
- *Commercial mixed use.* Primarily commercial area with up to 25 percent compatible residential uses above or adjacent.

Commercial

All commercial uses and purposes, including single- or multi-tenant retail, office, restaurant, entertainment, or professional uses.

Civic

All civic uses and purposes, including community centers, churches, post offices, and noncommercial public or social services.

Industrial

All industrial uses and purposes, including larger-scale manufacturing, distribution, storage, or transportation uses.

Table 2.1. Summary of Case Studies (in aproximate chronological order).

Referenced in chapter ◆

Color case, Chapter 2 •

	Introduction	Ch. 1 Green Neighborhoods	Ch. 3 Green Networks	Ch. 4 Gray Networks	Ch. 5 Gray Fabric	Ch. 6 Green Fabric	Ch. 7 Urban Water	Ch. 8 Getting to Green Neighborhoods
Radburn Radburn, New Jersey 1934 •	◆	◆		◆				
Village Homes Davis, California 1975	◆			◆				
Stapleton Denver, Colorado 1996 •				◆			◆	
Prairie Crossing Grayhurst, Illinois 1996							◆	
Playa Vista Los Angeles, California 1996 •								
Garrison Woods Calgary Alberta 1997						◆		
The Beach Toronto, Ontario 1998 •				◆				
Coffee Creek Chesterton, Indiana 1998 •							◆	
Orenco Station Hillsboro, Oregon 2000 •	◆				◆			
East Clayton Surrey, British Columbia 2002			◆					
Heritage Park Minneapolis, Minnesota 2002 •				◆			◆	
Royal Avenue Eugene, Oregon 2003		◆		◆				
Villebois Wilsonville, Oregon 2004 •			◆			◆		
South East False Creek Vancouver, British Columbia 2005				◆				◆

Open Space 17.2 acres 16%	Streets 16 acres 15%	Residential 55.2 acres 52%		Commercial 9.6 acres 9%	Mixed use 6 acres 6%	Civic/Industry 1.6 acres 2 %

106-acre study area, including 492 dwellings with a small commercial area, community pool, elementary school, and community open space. Initiated in 1928 but never fully built out. Gross density is 4.7 dwellings per acre.

Radburn is located in the suburban borough of Fair Lawn, New Jersey, with approximately 32,000 people, located 21 miles northwest of New York City.

Radburn was the first model Garden City to be developed in the United States. Although the design was originally conceived as a planned city of 30,000 people, only about 500 dwellings were constructed before the U.S. stock market crashed in 1929. This innovative plan was designed with the safety of children in mind and is said to have turned neighborhood design inside out by featuring a park system as the neighborhood "front." Also notable is a circulation system that separates major vehicular traffic from the primary pedestrian circulation, which is located in the parks.

Radburn is located at a commuter rail station and has at its center a modest shopping area and some apartment housing. The segregated pedestrian pathway system leads uninterrupted to the shopping area; however, street crossing is necessary in the commercial area. The vehicular circulation system, called a "superblock," was designed to keep the central area in parkland. Through roads are located on a grid of about 1,000 by 1,600 feet; within that grid, homes are located on narrow lanes. Pedestrian circulation interconnects the lane ends with the pathway system, creating a fine-grained pedestrian network.

Much of the Radburn neighborhood is allocated to shared, public open space that forms a hierarchical network interconnecting private yards, via narrow common pathways, to continuous public parks, schools, and a community pool.

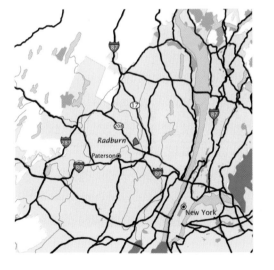

Credits

City Housing Corporation; Clarence S. Stein and Henry Wright, town planners

Radburn: Green Network

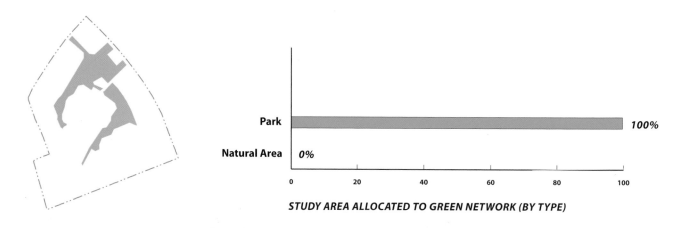

Park 100%

Natural Area 0%

STUDY AREA ALLOCATED TO GREEN NETWORK (BY TYPE)

(a)

(b)

(a) Interior parkland. Photo by K. Helphand. (b) Path leading to one of several street underpasses. (c) Edge conditions between yard and park: low fences and hedges mediate public and private. Photo by K. Helphand.

(c)

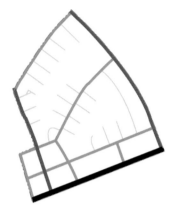

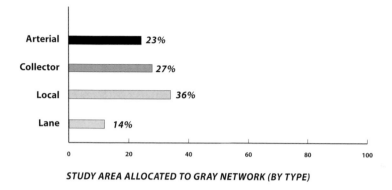

STUDY AREA ALLOCATED TO GRAY NETWORK (BY TYPE)

(a)

(b)

(a) Pedestrian paths alternate with cul-de-sacs to connect collector street edges to the interior park system. (b) One of the broader collector streets. Photo by K. Helphand. (c) Cul-de-sacs service the homes and are important social spaces. Photo by K. Helphand.

(c)

Radburn: Gray Fabric

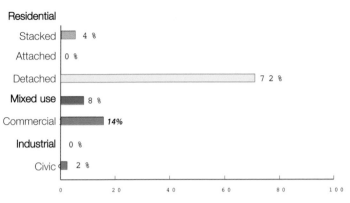

Residential

Stacked	4 %
Attached	0 %
Detached	7 2 %
Mixed use	8 %
Commercial	*14%*
Industrial	0 %
Civic	2 %

0   20   40   60   80   100

STUDY AREA ALLOCATED TO GRAY FABRIC (BY TYPE)

(a) Homes and yards enfront public spaces. (b) Radburn's commercial center. Photo by K. Helphand.

(a)

(b)

Stapleton

1,328-acre study area with 12,000 dwellings, a large commercial area, business parks, schools, recreation centers, and industrial and institutional uses. Partially constructed in 2004. Gross density is 9 dwellings per acre.

Open Space	Streets	Residential	Commercial	Mixed use	Civic/Industry
405 acres	235.2 acres	338 acres	267 acres	24 acres	59.2 acres
30%	18%	25%	20%	2%	4 %

Stapleton is located on the former Stapleton International Airport site in metropolitan Denver, Colorado, a rapidly growing area of 2.2 million people. Stapleton is in northeast Denver, 9 miles from downtown Denver.

Stapleton abuts mature residential areas of Denver. It is noted for its extensive system of parks and open spaces woven within a mixed-use community modeled after the street patterns and neighborhood character of Denver's older residential areas.

The master plan (as illustrated) calls for four planning zones, three mixed-use town centers, and a regional commercial center. The regional center, in the northwest quadrant of the plan, includes a mix of small and big box retail and offices. East 29th Town Center, near the first neighborhood and the older Denver residential areas, is laid out along a main street and includes an eclectic mix of shops, restaurants, and offices. A broad parkway connects this town center with the Westerly Creek Regional Greenway at the site's eastern edge. Apartment and row housing edge this parkway near the town center, and single-family homes line it to the east.

The open space system is a form-giving aspect of the Stapleton plan. Parks and boulevards within neighborhoods interconnect with natural areas in which eight High Plains habitat types will be restored. When restored, Westerly and Sand creeks will complete important links of a major regional greenway system, which will eventually connect to the Rocky Mountain Arsenal National Wildlife Refuge.

Credits

Stapleton Redevelopment Foundation and Forest City Development; Andropogon Associates Inc.; Civitas Inc., Denver; BRW Inc. Engineers

Stapleton: Green Network

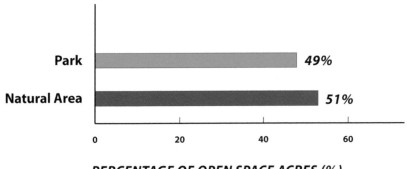

PERCENTAGE OF OPEN SPACE ACRES (%)

(a) Founders Green in Stapleton's First Neighborhood. (b) A small park designed to accommodate stormwater. (c) The restored Westerly Creek corridor along the eastern edge of the site.

(a)

(b)

(c)

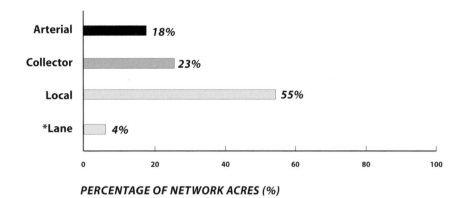

PERCENTAGE OF NETWORK ACRES (%)

(a)

(b)

(c)

Alley (a) and residential street (b) in Stapleton's First Neighborhood. (c) 29th Avenue extends Denver's traditional boulevard system.

Stapleton: Gray Fabric

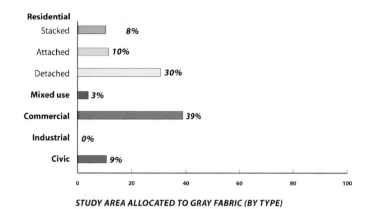

STUDY AREA ALLOCATED TO GRAY FABRIC (BY TYPE)

(a)

(b)

(a) and (b) Detached housing in the First Neighborhood. (c) Entrance to the regional retail center.

(c)

Playa Vista

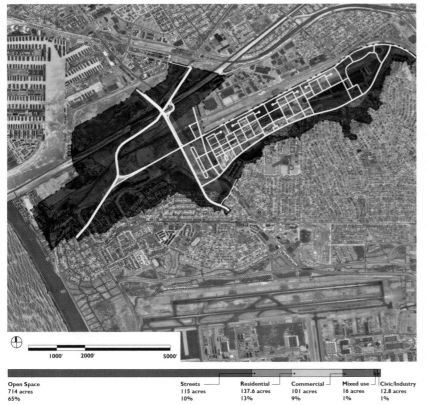

1,097-acre study area with 13,000 dwellings, many buildings with mixed uses, a mixed-use village center, entertainment and business districts, recreation centers, a school, and restored wetlands. Partially constructed in 2004. Gross density is 11.7 dwellings per acre.

| Open Space 714 acres 65% | Streets 115 acres 10% | Residential 137.6 acres 13% | Commercial 101 acres 9% | Mixed use 16 acres 1% | Civic/Industry 12.8 acres 1% |

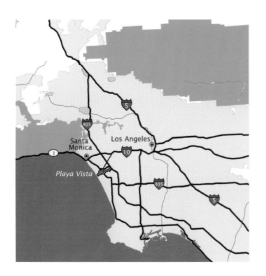

Playa Vista is located on the former Hughes Aircraft manufacturing site in metropolitan Los Angeles, California, an area of 12.4 million people. Playa Vista sits north of the Los Angeles airport and west of downtown Los Angeles.

Early planning for a development on the site, recognized as the last developable tract of land in central Los Angeles, began in 1985. After much community opposition and numerous design revisions, a plan that kept 65 percent of the site in open space was approved in 1993. Playa Vista is notable for its density, which is much higher than most contemporary new urbanist communities, with most of it in four- to five-story condominium buildings. A small percentage of residences are single-family, attached or detached homes.

Playa Vista comprises twelve districts, each centered around a small park and each with a distinctive architectural style. Small-scale commercial is allowed at street level in many areas, often adjacent to the parks. Office parks are situated within walking distance of the town center.

Much of the public opposition to the development involved how much of the Ballona wetlands and supporting habitat would be preserved or restored and in what way. Starting in 1978, the Friends of Ballona Wetlands, working to preserve and restore this last remnant tidal marsh in Los Angeles County, succeeded in having 340 acres of the wetlands protected. Additionally, methane gas is known to underlie the site—a public disaster waiting to happen, according to opponents. To prevent such a disaster, developers have used extensive measures to seal out the gas and wire the entire development with sensors and alarm systems.

Credits

Playa Capital Company; Legorretta Arquitectos; Moore Ruble Yudell; Duany Plater-Zyberk & Company; EDAW Inc.; Roma Design Group; Moule & Polyzoides

Playa Vista: Green Network

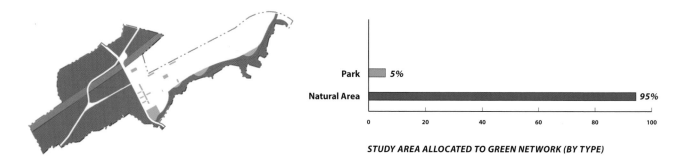

STUDY AREA ALLOCATED TO GREEN NETWORK (BY TYPE)

Park		5%
Natural Area		95%

(a)

(b)

(a) The park at the town center. (b) Concert Park in the Garden District. (c) The restored Ballona Wetlands compose the entire western portion of the site.

(c)

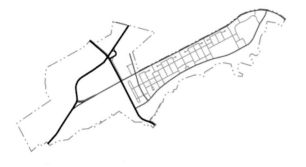

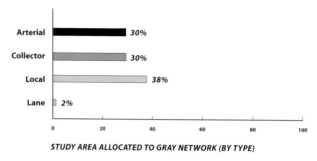

STUDY AREA ALLOCATED TO GRAY NETWORK (BY TYPE)

(a)

(a) A local street in the town center.
(b) A network of paths occurs mid-block throughout the neighborhoods. (c) Playa Vista Promenade interconnects community and neighborhood parks and the Ballona Wetlands.

(b)

(c)

Playa Vista: Gray Fabric

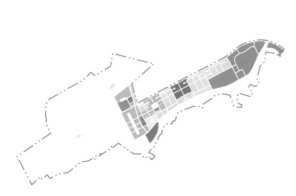

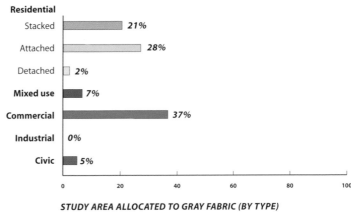

STUDY AREA ALLOCATED TO GRAY FABRIC (BY TYPE)

(a)

(b)

(a) and (b) Four story stacked–unit residential buildings over underground parking. Some buildings include office uses at grade. (c) Narrow public paths are heavily vegetated to maintain residential privacy.

(c)

The Beach

92-acre study area with 735 dwellings, located between a shopping and transit street and the beach. Mixed use along Queen Street and a range of building types and densities. Near completion in 2004. Gross density is 8 dwellings per acre.

Open Space	Streets	Residential	Commercial	Mixed use
35.8 acres	18.8 acres	31.1 acres	2.9 acres	3.1 acres
39%	20%	34%	3%	3%

The Beach, a redevelopment of the Greenwood Racetrack, is a new neighborhood and park located within the city of Toronto, Canada (metropolitan population, 4.7 million; City of Toronto population, 2.5 million). The new residential area is immediately west of the historic Beaches neighborhood, a nineteenth-century resort community known for eclectic shopping along Queen Street and a 5-mile boardwalk along the beach.

Roughly half of the site has been redeveloped as a park and an adjacent cinema complex, and the other half is the residential neighborhood. Streets in the neighborhood extend the existing grid from Queen Street to Lakeshore Boulevard, which runs along the waterfront, forming long view corridors and direct, easy pedestrian access to either destination. An east-west pedestrian path provides access to the park. Mixed-use buildings, with commercial at grade and condominium housing above, line Queen Street, a major east-west street and streetcar corridor extending through downtown Toronto. Each neighborhood street includes a mix of single-family, detached and duplex homes, all on narrow lots ranging from 18 to 24 feet wide. Building design was intended to complement the traditional styling of the adjacent neighborhood. Row houses and four-story apartment buildings are located along Lake Shore Boulevard near the beach.

The 28-acre park serves a much larger neighborhood. It includes a stormwater management pond, a habitat restoration area, and open grass and flower gardens and also provides several points of connection to the beach and its boardwalk, part of an extensive east-side trail system in Toronto.

Credits
Tribute Communities; Urban Strategies Inc.; City of Toronto

The Beach: Green Network

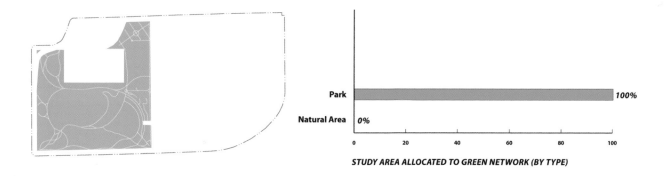

STUDY AREA ALLOCATED TO GREEN NETWORK (BY TYPE)

Park 100%
Natural Area 0%

(a) The 28 acre park west of the residential area serves several neighborhoods. The pond captures stormwater. (b) A constructed wetland provides wildlife habitat and cleans water.

(a)

(b)

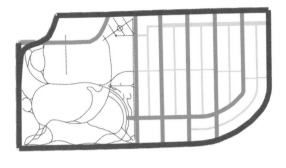

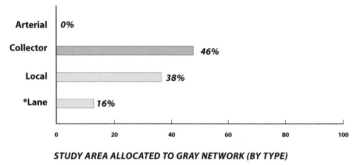

STUDY AREA ALLOCATED TO GRAY NETWORK (BY TYPE)

(a)

(b)

(c)

(a) Local streets connect Queen Street to the waterfront.
(b) The streetcar along Queen Street extends to and
through downtown Toronto. (c) The east–west path
between houses connects to the park.

The Beach: Gray Fabric

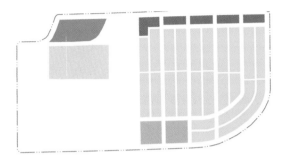

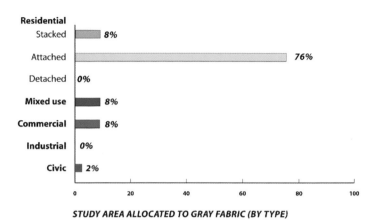

Residential

Stacked 8%
Attached 76%
Detached 0%
Mixed use 8%
Commercial 8%
Industrial 0%
Civic 2%

0   20   40   60   80   100

STUDY AREA ALLOCATED TO GRAY FABRIC (BY TYPE)

(a)

(b)

(a) Mixed use buildings mediate between the commercial edge along Queen Street, south-facing residential apartments and single family homes across the alley.
(b) Duplex "terrace" homes are mixed with similarly styled single family detached homes, and on another street, single family detached homes (c) are mixed with duplexes.

(c)

Coffee Creek Center

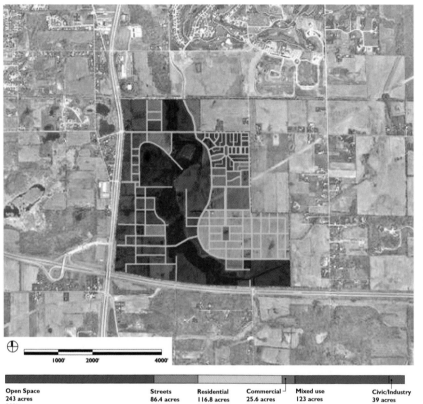

| Open Space 243 acres 38% | | | Streets 86.4 acres 14% | Residential 116.8 acres 18% | Commercial 25.6 acres 4% | Mixed use 123 acres 20% | | Civic/Industry 39 acres 6% |

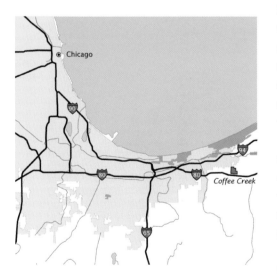

634-acre study area planned for 3,000 dwellings in a series of mixed-use neighborhoods, each with a commercial center, and situated around the Coffee Creek ecological preserve. Partially constructed in 2004. Gross density is 4.7 dwellings per acre.

Coffee Creek Center is located approximately 5 miles southeast of Chesterton in the Dunelands area of Indiana, at the intersection of two highways, Highway 49 and the Indiana Toll Road (Highway 80). The Dunelands communities have a population of 31,000.

Coffee Creek Center is an intentional, environmentally sensitive community that aims to be ecologically and economically sustainable. It is notable for catering to a work-at-home population and integrating the protection and restoration of the Coffee Creek Watershed Preserve at the center of the community. A grid street system is used, however, for environmental protection, few streets connect neighborhoods across the wetland. Coffee Creek Center is designed to be a series of compact, pedestrian- and bicycle-friendly neighborhoods, each with commercial and civic services and parks. The 4-million-square-foot downtown district, located adjacent to two highways, is intended to make the community economically self-sufficient by about 2015. All buildings will be designed to take advantage of daylighting and renewable energy, and sustainable materials will be used.

The 210-acre Coffee Creek preserve is significant for its major restoration of the pre-agriculture wetlands and upland prairie. The preserve is a conservation district independently managed by a conservancy group. With water considered to be the site's "lifeblood," a unique stormwater management system was designed to capture all runoff, filter it, store it, and slowly release it back to the groundwater.

Credits

Lake Erie Land Company; William McDonough and Partners; Looney Ricks Kiss and Gibbs Planning Group; Atelier Dreiseitl (water management consultants)

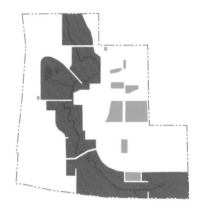

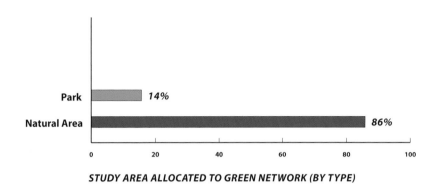

STUDY AREA ALLOCATED TO GREEN NETWORK (BY TYPE)

(a)

(b)

(a) Coffee Creek Preserve with a viewing structure at its edge. (b) and (c) Pedestrian paths extend into and across the preserve.

(c)

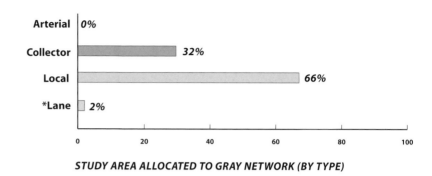

Arterial | 0%
Collector | 32%
Local | 66%
*Lane | 2%

STUDY AREA ALLOCATED TO GRAY NETWORK (BY TYPE)

(a)

(b)

(c)

(a) The northern collector street crosses the preserve.
(b) A street in the future Village Green. (c) The
pedestrian promenade extends from the Village Green
to the edge of the preserve.

Coffee Creek Center: Gray Fabric

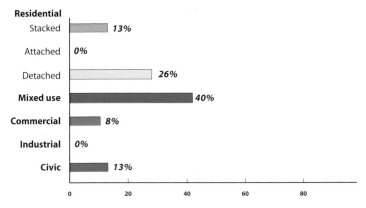

Residential

- Stacked — *13%*
- Attached — *0%*
- Detached — *26%*
- **Mixed use** — *40%*
- **Commercial** — *8%*
- **Industrial** — *0%*
- **Civic** — *13%*

STUDY AREA ALLOCATED TO GRAY FABRIC (BY TYPE)

(a)

(b)

(c)

(a) and (b) Single family detached and attached (duplex) homes are located adjacent to each other.
(c) Stacked dwellings.

Orenco Station

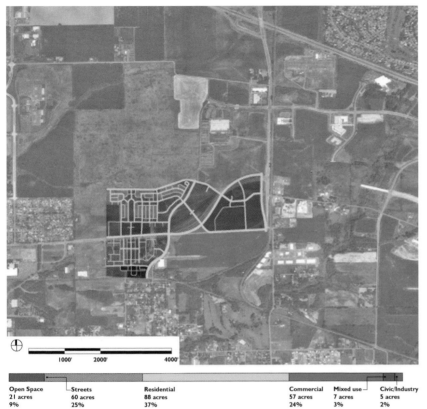

Open Space
21 acres
9%

Streets
60 acres
25%

Residential
88 acres
37%

Commercial
57 acres
24%

Mixed use
7 acres
3%

Civic/Industry
5 acres
2%

156-acre study area planned for 1,835 dwellings and a mixed-use commercial center at build out. Initiated in 1995 and substantially constructed in 2004. Gross density is about 12 dwellings per acre.

Orenco Station is located in Hillsboro, Oregon, a rapidly growing suburban community of 75,000 (also known as "Silicon Forest") on the western side of the 460-square-mile Portland metropolitan area (population 1.3 million), about 10 miles from downtown Portland.

Orenco Station was named for an early-twentieth-century company town of the Oregon Nursery Company. Sited at a Tri-Met MAX light rail station opened in 1998, it was the first new, transit-oriented development on this light rail line. The plan, which integrates compact development and transportation management with the scale and character of traditional neighborhood elements, has been widely recognized as a model of transit-driven, pedestrian-scale development.

The plan is organized around Orenco Station Parkway, which connects the light rail station on the south side of an arterial road along a "main street" in the town center to the principal park at the north end. A fine-grained gridded network of narrow local streets forms a walkable pattern of residential blocks throughout the 190-acre residential area. Along these streets is a mix of uses and densities characteristic of a new urbanist village. The urban design of the town center, reflecting historic downtown buildings, provides a strong identity for the development.

Orenco Station's park system includes approximately 5 acres of maintained parks. The larger Central Park terminates the main shopping street of the town center. Two neighborhood parks provide a spatial and recreational focus to adjacent residential areas.

Credits

Pacific Realty Associates (PacTrust); Costa Pacific Homes; Fletcher Farr Ayotte Architecture Planning Interiors; Iverson Associates; Alpha Engineering; Walker Macy Landscape Architects

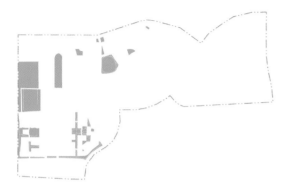

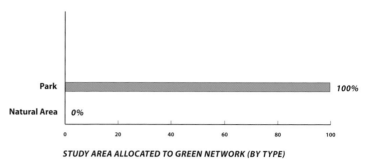

STUDY AREA ALLOCATED TO GREEN NETWORK (BY TYPE)

(a)

(b)

(a) Single family detached and attached homes encircle the central park. (b) A small gathering space at the northern end of Central Park. (c) From the park, a view south through Main Street to the light rail station.

(c)

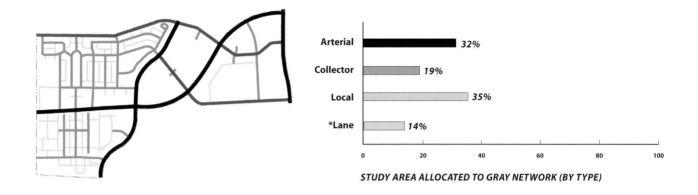

STUDY AREA ALLOCATED TO GRAY NETWORK (BY TYPE)

Arterial 32%
Collector 19%
Local 35%
*Lane 14%

(a)

(b)

(c)

(a) The Trimet light rail station at Orenco Station. (b) The pedestrian space along Main Street. (c) A local street.

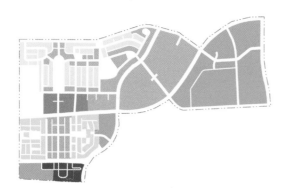

Residential

Stacked	36%
Attached	9%
Detached	12%
Mixed use	5%
Commercial	36%
Industrial	3%
Civic	3%

STUDY AREA ALLOCATED TO GRAY FABRIC (BY TYPE)

(a) Attached housing adjacent to the park. (b) Live-work buildings in the town center. (c) A mixed use (commercial, office, residential) building on Main Street.

(a)

(b)

(c)

Heritage Park

256-acre study area with 900 dwellings, public and private schools, social service centers, and churches, with industry at the north and south ends. Partially redeveloped in 2004. Gross density is 3.5 dwellings per acre.

Open Space	Streets	Residential	Mixed use	Civic/Industry
28 acres	53.6 acres	90.4 acres	6.4 acres	77.2 acres
11%	21%	35%	3%	30%

Heritage Park is located in a former public housing area near downtown Minneapolis, Minnesota, a city of 383,000 in a metropolitan area of 2.3 million.

Heritage Park is a mixed-use, mixed-income neighborhood redeveloped on the site of Minneapolis's first large public housing project. Redeveloped parks and a central greenway spine at the heart of new residential areas help to connect two subneighborhoods split by a high-volume roadway. Planning incorporated extensive public involvement and is phased to allow the rehousing of the former public housing residents.

Parks and schools form the neighborhood centers, and a commercial center is planned at the southeast corner of the development. The housing is mixed, single-family; duplex; and small townhouse units, including both rental and for-sale units. A fine-grained network of streets and alleys was added to the coarse-grained network of the former public housing projects. Roughly situated over the former alignment of the deeply buried Bassett Creek is a north-south boulevard and greenway. Conceived as a Bassett Creek resurfacing project, the greenway is a defining public amenity that also serves an important stormwater function. In addition to providing public open space and walkways, the stormwater "gardens" in Heritage Park treat and detain runoff from about 400 acres of the city.

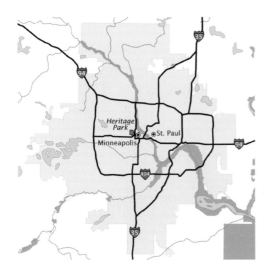

Credits

McCormack Baron and Legacy Management, lead developer; Urban Design Associates; SRF Consulting Group; early conceptual plans by Design Center for the American Urban Landscape

Heritage Park: Green Network

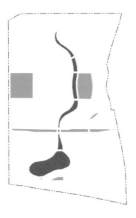

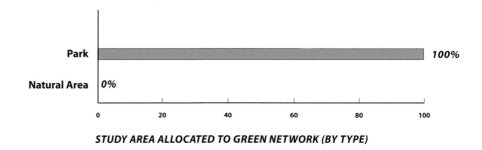

Park   **100%**

Natural Area   **0%**

0   20   40   60   80   100

STUDY AREA ALLOCATED TO GREEN NETWORK (BY TYPE)

(a)

(b)

(a) Housing along Van White Memorial Boulevard
overlooks the greenway and stormwater gardens.
(b) Drainage swales along the greenway, the re-surfaced
Basset Creek, slow and filter stormwater runoff.
(c) Pedestrian paths wind through the greenway.

(c)

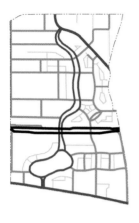

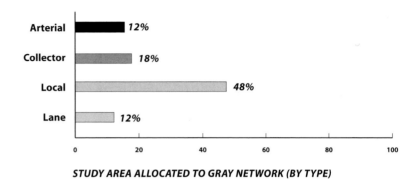

Arterial		12%
Collector		18%
Local		48%
Lane		12%

STUDY AREA ALLOCATED TO GRAY NETWORK (BY TYPE)

(a)

(b)

(c)

(a) Van White Memorial Boulevard forms the edges of the public greenway. (b) A local access road to multi-family housing. (c) A pedestrian and bicycle path along the greenway.

Heritage Park: Gray Fabric

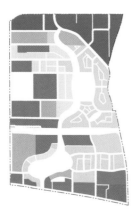

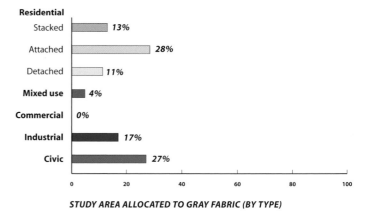

STUDY AREA ALLOCATED TO GRAY FABRIC (BY TYPE)

Residential	
Stacked	13%
Attached	28%
Detached	11%
Mixed use	4%
Commercial	0%
Industrial	17%
Civic	27%

(a)

(b)

(a) and (b) Row housing set in close proximity to the sidewalk conserves land and puts eyes on the street. (c) A single family duplex (attached) home.

(c)

Villebois

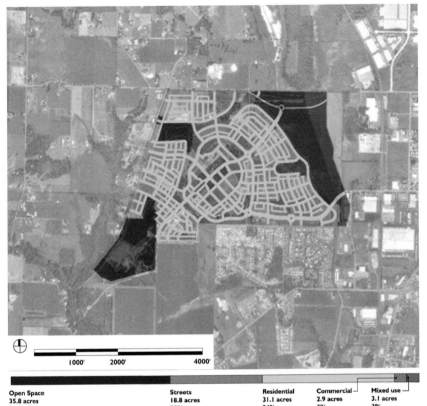

Open Space	Streets	Residential	Commercial	Mixed use
35.8 acres	18.8 acres	31.1 acres	2.9 acres	3.1 acres
39%	20%	34%	3%	3%

482-acre study area planned for 2,300 dwellings, a mixed-use commercial center, and a public elementary school at build out. Partially constructed in 2004. Gross density is 4.8 dwellings per acre.

Villebois is located in Wilsonville, Oregon, a rapidly growing suburban community of 14,000 at the southern tip of the Portland metropolitan area (population 1.3 million), about 20 miles from downtown Portland.

Villebois, roughly translated as "village near the woods," is named for the area's French Prairie heritage and the small European town urbanism to which it aspires. This plan for the wooded hilltop site of a former state hospital has been shaped by some of the developers and planners of nearby Orenco Station. It integrates compact development principles with protecting environmental assets, managing stormwater, and enhancing urban forest.

Sited on a hilltop, the Village Center is a high-density, mixed-use district situated at a crossroads where three smaller, nested neighborhoods overlap. The Village Center will provide commercial, recreational, and educational services. At its heart is a half-acre urban plaza, sited to preserve a large, mature tree. A circumnavigating, pedestrian-scaled loop road links off-site transit and the three adjacent neighborhoods with the Village Center.

The natural environment and environmental functions are prominent. While restoring the historic drainage pattern of the predevelopment site, the plan also adapts the form and organization of landscape and urban design elements (e.g., parks, street medians, and planting strips) and natural areas to serve stormwater management functions, including conveyance, filtration, infiltration, and detention. Significant efforts have been made to preserve existing trees.

Credits
Costa Pacific Communities; Alpha Engineering Inc.; Walker Macy; Fletcher Farr Ayotte; Iverson Associates

Villebois: Green Network

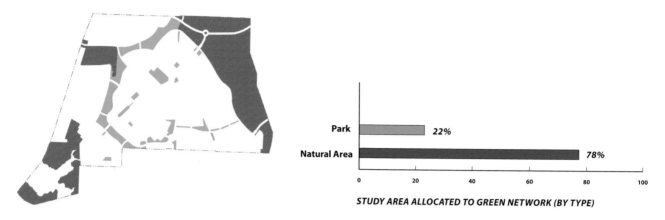

STUDY AREA ALLOCATED TO GREEN NETWORK (BY TYPE)

Park 22%

Natural Area 78%

(a)

(b)

(a) A grove of trees will be the site of one neighborhood park. (b) The greenway includes a re-surfaced creek, will provide stormwater functions, and will be a recreational corridor.

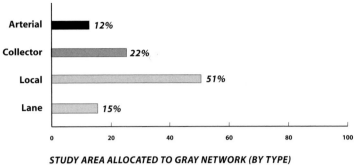

Arterial	12%
Collector	22%
Local	51%
Lane	15%

STUDY AREA ALLOCATED TO GRAY NETWORK (BY TYPE)

(a)

(b)

(a) The village center will occur at the intersection of two collector roads. (b) and (c) Some existing roads will be restored and several new local streets will be aligned with rows of existing trees—both efforts to preserve the site's urban forest.

(c)

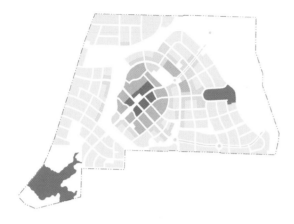

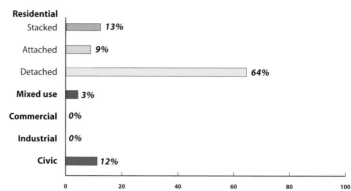

Residential		
Stacked		13%
Attached		9%
Detached		64%
Mixed use		3%
Commercial		0%
Industrial		0%
Civic		12%

(a)

(b)

(a) The Village Center square is designed around a massive existing tree. (b) Density will be concentrated in mixed use buildings at the Village Center. (c) Existing buildings will be re-used for office, educational, and recreational uses.

(c)

Chapter 3
Green Networks

Urban river and stream networks can become an essential structuring element of a city, can be beautiful, and can be the sustenance of a rich urban ecology.

W. E. Wenk, "Toward an Inclusive Concept of Infrastructure"

Urban green spaces include everything in cities that has vegetation. Either natural or planted, green spaces range from potted plants to forests. Through green spaces, people relate to nature in the city. Urban green spaces currently serve many important ecological roles, but they can be designed and managed to do it far better. They can cleanse and return water to the ground, where natural rainfall should go. They can mitigate the urban heat island and reduce the need to heat and cool buildings. They can provide habitat for urban wildlife. They can clean the common pollutants associated with vehicles and roads, both by taking up some of the gases associated with air pollution and by cleaning stormwater runoff. Finally, their green wastes, such as yard debris, can be composted and used to rebuild urban soils.

As a term, "urban green space" is roughly analogous to the more commonly used term "open space," by which most people mean undeveloped land or land without buildings, roads, and parking. Viewed positively, the terms refer to yards, parks, greenways, and natural areas. However, the term "open space" is perhaps a problem. Taken literally, "open space" implies absence— places left open or vacant in the spatial fabric of a city. Some open spaces are indeed just that. But they are also much more, and the term encompasses a far greater diversity of types, sizes, shapes, and functions than its simplicity implies. Open space might be your yard, the park, the playfields or the garden down the street, the square at the town center, the river corridor that runs through town, or the prairie at the edge. It might be "open" but also complex and highly developed (engineered and built) to perform particular recreational, aesthetic, agricultural, practical, or ecological functions. Open spaces can and do support a diversity of human uses as well as environmental functions, and their vitality influences quality of life as much as it does the integrity of land, air, and water and forest resources. They do environmental work (Figure 3.1; Table 3.1).

In recent years, landscape architects have drawn attention to the fundamental role of urban open spaces to reestablish the hydrological balance that is seriously impaired in most cities.[1] Planners and ecologists have argued for its equally important role in reestablishing healthy wildlife habitat.[2] A city's green spaces can and should be employed to harness natural processes in the service of the urban environment. They can serve as "working landscapes" to clean sewage and urban runoff; clean, store, and infiltrate rainwater in ponds and wetlands; and provide space for flooding while also offering beauty, respite, wildlife habitat, and recreation.

The term "green infrastructure" has become a popular catchphrase used to refer to the environmental services or work of urban landscapes. In 1999, the (U.S.) President's Council on Sus-

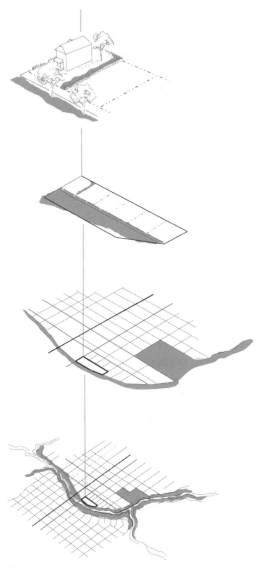

Figure 3.1 Green networks shown across scales.

Table 3.1. Open Spaces across Scales

Scale	Example
Lot	Yards
	Courts
Block	Play lots
	Commons
	Pocket parks
Street	Rights of way
	Medians
	Planting strips
Neighborhood	School yards
	Neighborhood parks
	Playgrounds
	Drainageways
Community	Community parks
	Play fields
	Smaller conservation area
	Greenways
Region	Regional parks
	Large conservation areas
	Greenways
	Waterways

tainable Development defined green infrastructure as "the network of open spaces, airsheds, watersheds, woodlands, wildlife habitat, parks, and other natural areas that provides many vital services that sustain life and enrich the quality of life."[3] Although this definition was not specific to urban areas, urban foresters have used "green infrastructure" to refer to the environmental services that urban forests provide to cities.[4] Conservationists Mark Benedict and Ed McMahon define green infrastructure as "an interconnected network of green space that conserves natural ecosystem values and functions and provides associated benefits to human populations."[5] This definition is somewhat parallel to what landscape ecologists would call the urban landscape's "ecological structure" (discussed later in this chapter). Various other disciplines are picking up the term "green infrastructure" to suggest equal value for landscapes as for gray infrastructure such as sewers and roads—or, conversely, to suggest the greening of conventional gray infrastructure. If "infrastructure" is the underlying framework that provides vital services for the city and if "green" is a contemporary colloquialism that means environmentally friendly or healthy, then a better definition for "green infrastructure" could be the green framework that performs a multitude of vital environmental services in cities.

With this broad, inclusive definition for "green infrastructure" in mind, we use the term "green networks" to refer to the geography of open spaces, such as parks, greenways, and natural areas. "Green networks" is narrower in definition than "green infrastructure," because these spaces are predominantly the public realm and, as such, are important elements of land use and community planning and design. "Green networks" as a term and a concept is flexible and encompassing. While it primarily includes the urban elements of parks, greenways, and natural areas, it might also include many other green elements, such as parkways, green streets, and utility and drainage corridors that serve environmental as well as human purposes. Green networks can be seen, mapped, and traversed by people and animals and, thus, experienced and appreciated. They are physical elements of the city that can be planned for alongside streets and development. In ideal circumstances, green networks are the urban version of Benedict and McMahon's "interconnected network of green space that conserves natural ecosystem values and functions and provides

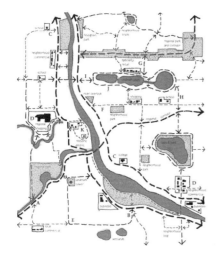

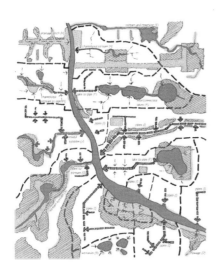

Figure 3.2 A disconnected open space network (top) and a proposal to interconnect the same network (bottom). (Source: Design Centre for the American Urban Landscape, University of Minnesota)

associated benefits to human populations."[6] In actual fact, the green networks of most neighborhoods and cities are piecemeal and fragmented, although many cities aspire toward more interconnected systems of public open spaces (Figure 3.2).

If green networks are understood to be a city's public open spaces, then "green infrastructure" can be used to refer to the entirety of urban green spaces. Green infrastructure would include public open spaces, the urban forest that extends throughout the city, and the private landscapes of commerce, industry, and homes. Green infrastructure describes function. It is, as planner Timothy Beatley describes, all of the working landscapes in cities that serve significant infrastructure-like roles, including mitigating air pollution, cleaning water, and controlling floods.[7] The green infrastructure does part of the work of running a city and helps to make the city less dependent on its region for water and waste disposal in particular. Infrastructure, whether gray or green, has never been conceived or designed to serve ecological functions; however, this may be one of our biggest oversights of the past and one of our best opportunities for the future. The services of nature in the city have great potential. As we study cities from an ecological perspective, it becomes clear that a green infrastructure, which explicitly serves natural functions, is needed to make cities more sustainable.[8] This, in turn, suggests an ecologically based approach to city planning and building as a whole.

Fragmented Systems

The history of parks in North America includes many important lessons as well as visionary works by notable landscape architects and planners, including Frederick Law Olmsted, the Olmsted Brothers, George Kessler, H.W.S. Cleveland, and Charles Elliot. Boston's Emerald Necklace, designed by Frederick Law Olmsted from 1878 to 1890, is generally recognized as the first interconnected park system in North America.[9] It was also the first green network intentionally designed to solve flood and water pollution problems while also serving recreation and civic purposes. Other plans soon followed, including ones for Minneapolis (H.W.S. Cleveland; see Figure 3.3), Buffalo (F. L. Olmsted), and Kansas City (George Kessler), and twenty years later, for Seattle

(Olmsted Bros.), Cincinnati (Kessler), and Portland, Oregon (J. C. Olmsted).[10] Most of these plans took advantage of existing natural resources—such as river corridors, lakes, and hilltops—for aesthetic, social, and recreational purposes. Although not driven primarily by environmental concerns, the landscape architects nonetheless saw both human and natural values in creating interconnected green networks.

Visionary park system planning, land acquisition, and development work in North American cities was nearly halted during the Great Depression and World War II, save for projects done by the Civilian Conservation Corps and the Work Projects Administration. In the early postwar period, suburbanization outpaced the ability of most cities and counties to plan for and acquire land for parks systems. In 1962, the Outdoor Recreation Review Commission reported that America's population was outgrowing its outdoor resources.[11] The early 1970s saw a brief rekindling of interest in interconnected park systems, but soon thereafter cuts in the Land and Water Conservation Fund by the Carter administration and the recession of 1982 put an end to that movement.[12] In 1985 the President's Commission on Americans Outdoors once again emphasized the value of interconnected greenways and proposed a national system of greenways within and between cities. Some cities embarked on greenway programs in the early 1990s, but it was not until environmental imperatives of the later 1990s, such as the implementation of the EPA's urban stormwater management program, added urgency that many more cities once again began to plan urban greenways. In the meantime, the rapid and extensive expansion of urbanized areas had broadly affected ecosystems in their surrounding regions.

Sprawling urban development has also contributed to the most significant ecological problems of the twenty-first century: habitat loss, habitat fragmentation, and the related loss of ecological biodiversity.[13] For example, the U.S Geological Survey estimated that wetlands in the United States were lost at a rate of more than 60 acres per hour for the two hundred years from 1780 to 1990. California has lost 91 percent of its wetlands. The U.S. Fish and Wildlife Service estimated a net loss of 117,000 acres per year of wetlands from 1985 to 1995, 21 percent as a result of urban development.[14] In Oregon, no significant areas of

Figure 3.3 Minneapolis park system designed by H.W.S. Cleveland. (Source: Heckscher and Robinson, *Open Spaces*)

the original oak savanna habitat that once covered the Willamette Valley remain.[15] While much of this loss can be attributed to agriculture, urban development of these landscapes clearly plays a role as well.

Urban development contributes to the fragmentation of ecosystems because it separates habitat patches and breaks ecological connectivity.[16] For example, in the Willamette Valley in Oregon, the state's three largest cities—Eugene-Springfield, Salem, and metropolitan Portland—straddle the Willamette River. Riparian habitat has been reduced to little or nothing along many urbanized portions of the river, fragmenting the riparian corridor along its length.[17] At the same time, development has separated the forested uplands and many remaining wetland areas from the primary ecological corridor of the valley, the Willamette River.

Engaging Landscape Ecology

An ecologically based approach to city building, one that begins with an understanding of cities as a part of nature, engages nature and natural processes to help sustain the city. Taking this approach to city planning implies "moving beyond separate visions for human and nature while recognizing that humans are a key species in contemporary earth ecosystems,"[18] or, as architect William McDonough says, cities could be places *of* nature.[19] In other words, an ecological approach views human ecology and natural ecology as interacting partners in the local ecosystem.

Such an approach to the design and planning of urban systems would allow natural processes to continue in a more ecologically healthy state, would produce fewer negative impacts on the urban environment itself and the surrounding region, and, particularly, would recycle urban wastes, all while also allowing for the healthy sustenance of its human populations. Timothy Beatley calls this approach "green urbanism," which he points out is a "*different* new urbanism, a new urbanism that is dramatically more ecological in design and functioning and that has ecological limits at its core."[20] A common example of this approach includes recycling programs for both manufactured and green urban wastes. In this case, the energy embodied in these materials is recycled within the urban ecosystem, not exported to another more rural ecosystem that cannot use it. Contemporary, and still experimental, water management programs that reuse gray water or that clean and infiltrate stormwater runoff help to maintain the urban ecosystem's water balance, reducing the need to import clean water and export polluted water.

To take an ecological approach to designing and managing the urban environment, each city's unique landscape ecology must be understood. Whereas ecology is the deep study of individual ecosystems or populations, landscape ecology is the broad study of heterogeneous land areas composed of a cluster of interacting ecosystems.[21] Landscape ecology studies three characteristics of landscapes: *structure,* or the spatial relationships among the distinctive ecosystems or landscape elements present; *function,* or the interactions among the spatial elements, such as flows of energy, materials, and species; and *change,* or the alterations in landscape structure or function over time.[22] The city is a unique ecosystem, derived from historic landscapes yet changed by urban structures and processes. The complexity and the vast extent of the urban environment coupled with its rate of change and the need to get ahead of that change makes this discipline appropriate for studying urban landscapes.

Landscape structure is the pattern and relationships among the many landscape elements or individual ecosystems that make up a larger, more complex landscape. Landscape structure can be seen from the air and, as such, can be mapped and measured. It is composed of the overall or predominant matrix, which is interrupted by patches of different habitat types or areas and connected by linear corridors. In the rural landscape—the focus of many of landscape ecology's founding studies—the predominant matrix would be cultivated fields interrupted by patches of habitat, such as forests and wetlands, that are interconnected with corridors, such as riparian corridors and hedgerows.[23] In the city, the landscape matrix is urban development interrupted by similar remnant habitat patches (e.g., forests and wetlands) that are interconnected with corridors, such as riparian corridors, drainage ditches, and utility corridors. The effective ecological structure of the city, the patches and corridors of natural landscapes, would roughly equate to the green networks described in this book.

Green Networks and Form

Landscape structure is a useful planning tool.[24] Much of the work in urban land use planning involves identifying patterns of development or preservation and the allowable uses for particular parcels of land. Setting aside lands for their important ecological functions remains a fledgling process, one struggling against a legal history that protects individual property rights and previously projected monetary values. In the United States, such federal laws as the Clean Water Act and the Endangered Species Act have allowed protection of habitat and water resources to become a part of urban planning in many cities.

Some urban ecologists are developing methods to prioritize those remaining elements of landscape structure and process that, taken together, are vital to the long-term health of the urban ecosystem. Conservation organizations such as the Nature Conservancy often focus on saving whatever vestiges of endangered or threatened species that exist. However, some argue that—from a planning perspective—a longer-term view toward ecosystem sustenance may be more important. In *Planning for Biodiversity,* Sheila Peck suggests that at the landscape scale, conserving representative samples of community types as well as functional relationships and physical connections among them is most important.[25] Preserving large blocks of remaining open space and preserving the opportunity for disturbance and hydrologic processes to continue are also high priorities for protection. Within this broad range, certain landscape types have been recognized as special priorities; for example, "species-rich" and viable natural areas may be of highest priority. Species-rich landscapes are most commonly riparian and wetland areas in which water is available and which contain a complexity of vegetation and of wildlife species. Viable natural areas are areas that contain primarily native species and that require little human input to sustain them.[26] Within these broad parameters, an ecological planning methodology would engage both scientists and the general population to help identify and prioritize the essential natural areas deemed worthy of conservation.[27]

Beginning with a full understanding of the ecological structure, functions, and processes of an urban ecosystem would be the preferable approach to initiating ecologically based planning for a city. Unfortunately, full knowledge of an urban ecosystem is typically considered unachievable because of ongoing planning and development. In every city, innumerable parallel planning efforts are under way at any given time, including planning for land use, transportation, infrastructure, economic development, and open space. Although ecologists might argue that ecosystem planning should occur first, it rarely leads these efforts.[28] Perhaps the first task in urban ecological planning is to create a sketch of the urban area's ecological structure as represented by the remaining riparian corridors, wetlands, meadows, and forests. Natural hazard areas, such as floodplains, landslide areas, or earthquake faults, may also be included. The resulting sketch—reviewed and refined through public process and adopted as an open space vision by representative agencies—would become a framework for various deeper studies, for protection and restoration efforts, and for multifunctional planning of many aspects of urban development (Figure 3.4).

Figure 3.4 Diagram of Eugene-Springfield, Oregon: ecological structure at the metropolitan scale.

A city's riparian corridors might be seen as the "trunk lines" of the city's green networks. Although reduced in area, fragmented, and often invaded by nonnative plants and animals, these corridors usually are highly valued by urban populations and also serve important hydrological and habitat functions. They are fragments of the landscape's former structure, still needed to perform the work that much more extensive natural areas once did. Riparian areas are linear, and as such they typically also provide connectivity between larger habitat patches. This contributes to the long-term viability of populations, particularly in fragmented landscapes such as cities.[29]

Planning efforts that study the ecological structure of the urban region and develop plans for metropolitan-scale green networks can guide green network planning at the city, neighborhood, and site scale. Within the context of the region, each city, each urban watershed, each neighborhood, and each site can create a vision for a greener future. In Portland, Oregon, the Metropolitan Greenspaces Program is working successfully toward preserving key armatures of the region's ecological structure, including riparian areas, wetlands, and upland forests. The program grew out of an initiative by the Portland Audubon Society in the late 1980s to establish an interconnected system of natural areas primarily to support wildlife habitat. This vision was coupled with

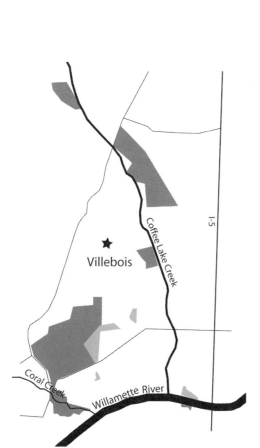

Villebois

Coffee Lake Creek

I-5

Coral Creek

Willamette River

■ Metro Land
■ Other Public Land

Figure 3.5 Diagram of protected resource lands adjacent to the Villebois site in Wilsonville, Oregon. (Source: derived from Metro, *Metro's Open Spaces Land Acquisition Report to Citizens*)

other local open space initiatives, and a first step in the process, a natural resources inventory, was done by Metro, the regional planning and public services district. By 1991, the vision had become an official program of Metro, and the multi-objective Metropolitan Greenspaces Program was born. A master plan was completed in 1992, and after one false start, a major land acquisition bond measure was passed in 1995.[30] Clearly rooted in the original vision of preserving a metropolitan area–wide, interconnected system of natural habitat areas, the program's goals also now include preserving the diversity of plant and animal life, restoring natural areas in heavily built up neighborhoods, establishing an interconnected trail system, and encouraging environmental awareness and public knowledge about the regional green spaces.

Between 1995 and 2001, Metro either purchased outright or otherwise protected through easements nearly 7,000 acres of natural areas throughout the region, including wetlands, riparian areas, forests, and meadows. The program now boasts an extensive list of partners, including virtually all of the counties and cities in the Metro region. Guided by the natural resources inventory and the Metropolitan Greenspaces Masterplan, these local jurisdictions and some independent land trusts have acquired additional lands to help complete the green network. While far from encompassing a protected and fully interconnected ecological structure, Portland is well on its way to reaching its goals, with significant segments of the many target areas now under public ownership or otherwise protected. In 2003, the Greenspaces Masterplan was being updated and two narrower plans—water quality and floodplain protection plan and a fish and wildlife habitat protection plan—were being developed.[31]

The visionary framework provided at the regional scale by the Greenspaces Masterplan has had a direct impact at the city and neighborhood scales. Villebois, a redevelopment project under construction in the suburban city of Wilsonville, south of Portland (see the case study in Chapter 2), provides an example of a smart growth community that engaged the Metropolitan Greenspaces vision and incorporated restoring landscape and making ecological connections into its plans (Figure 3.5). The Villebois project sits at the southern edge of the Tonquin Geologic target area of the Metropolitan Greenspaces Program. The area includes unique historic geologic features sculpted by ancient glacial flooding. Coffee Lake basin is the dominant natural feature targeted by the plan for acquisition, and portions of it immediately north of the Villebois site have been purchased by Metro. Land south of the Villebois site, called the Wilsonville tract, which would help to connect the Coffee Lake lands to the Willamette River corridor, are also owned by Metro, allowing the development project to make important ecological connections.[32] In addition to protecting more of the Coffee Lake wetlands, the development plan includes a broad greenway designed to connect the Coffee Lake wetlands and the Wilsonville tract at the south. Together, the Coffee Lake area, the Villebois greenway, and the Wilsonville tract comprise more than 500 acres of wetlands, riparian corridors, and upland forests located in a rapidly suburbanizing area (Figure 3.6). The plan exhibits a rare and relatively recent phenomenon of intentionally using redevelopment projects to restore and reconnect ecological structure.

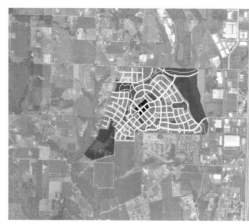

Figure 3.6 Villebois plan shown in context.

Connecting Region to Neighborhood

Landscape ecological studies can be conducted at nested scales. In the urban environment, these might start with the landscape region in which the city resides and progressively go down in scale to the metropolitan area, the major drainage basins, the districts or subdrainage basins, and the neighborhoods. The cross-scaled nature of such studies can inform the cross-scaled nature of urban planning and design, in which only certain questions are addressed at the regional or metropolitan scale and others are addressed at the city or neighborhood scale. What may be considered essential ecological structure at the metropolitan scale, for example, may in fact be destination habitat patches at the district scale. Patches and corridors that clearly exist and have ecological value at the neighborhood scale may be too insignificant to consider at the metropolitan scale. For example, a small grouping of native trees (a patch) and vegetated drainage swales (corridors) that are found at the neighborhood scale may hold no importance at the metropolitan scale, yet these small vestiges of habitat and corridor may contribute significantly to the overall functioning of the urban landscape by providing otherwise nonexistent connections.

Within and among the metropolitan region's ecological structures lies the fabric of the city. Planning and designing neighborhoods involves the detailed layout of this fabric, including the green and gray networks and the development parcels between them. In the United States and Canada, development occurs primarily in the private sector. Within a general land use and transportation framework of geography and policy, developers typically do the detailed planning that occurs at the neighborhood scale. Local governments can guide the physical form of neighborhoods through policy, regulation, and incentives, and in some cases local governments perform detailed advanced planning to demonstrate how to carry out policy. This neighborhood scale of planning and design is the focus of this book. It is where great potential exists to integrate or merge the green and the gray.

At the scale of the neighborhood, functioning natural areas should be protected and, where possible, interconnected with a region's ecological structure, such as rivers and large natural areas. Isolated patches of habitat (e.g., minor wetlands, remnant forests, or meadows) can be connected using the neighborhood's green network, drainage and power corridors, greenways, bikeways, and other linear parks. If designed to engage nature and natural processes, these green networks can contribute to the ecological functioning and health of the neighborhood. Added together, heterogeneous "bits of nature" (such as a patch of native trees) connected by green networks contribute far more significantly to regional ecosystems.[33] At the same time, they provide invaluable resources for residents.

While the larger-scaled ecological structure in urban areas may well serve primarily ecological functions, neighborhood-scale green networks, finely woven into the urban fabric, must serve many varied roles equally. As William Wenk says, the complexity of contemporary cities places a higher responsibility on public open space to serve multiple civic functions.[34] If the whole of the city's green network is understood to include a multiplicity of public green space—such as parks, school grounds, remnant natural areas, bikeways, drainage corridors, utility corridors, and even some streets—the primary role of each space will differ. For example, although its primary role may be channeling stormwater, a drainage corridor can also clean polluted water as well as provide civic improvement, public accessibility, education, and habitat. Wenk's design for stormwater gardens along the greenway at Heritage Park, pictured here, does exactly that (Figure 3.7). Urban green spaces, which should be dedicated to multiple uses and defined broadly, will likely require the partnership of numerous city agencies to create and manage them.

Using an ecologically based approach would allow neighborhood designers not only to understand and address a site in its social, economic, transportation, and land use contexts but also to study its current or potential contributions to larger-scaled ecological structure and functions as well as its ability to mitigate the development's future environmental impacts. The site itself, or the local context, may suggest opportunities for the neighborhood's green infrastructure that may, in turn, help to shape the neighborhood's layout. For example, degraded agricultural ditches or a fragment of a former stream corridor may provide the inspiration and incentive for restoring riparian corridors and a healthy local hydrology.

In one example, remnant ditches, headwater streams, and wetland—as well as an important hydrological position in the landscape—all pointed toward planning a surface drainage system for the East Clayton neighborhood in Surrey, British Columbia. In this plan, streets, parkways, multi-use green corridors, stormwater wetlands, protected riparian zones, parks, and school yards all work together to form an interconnected green network aimed at diminishing the typical impacts of new development on water systems (Figure 3.8). The plan, prepared in 2000 by the University of British Columbia James Taylor Chair in Landscape and Liveable Environments for the City of Surrey, was developed with a specific intent of demonstrating sustainable development principles, addressing Greater Vancouver's Livable Region Strategic Plan, and protecting the Green Zone (described below).[35] The site is located upstream of two of the region's significant natural resources, the Nicomekl and Serpentine rivers, both of which flow into Boundary Bay, a significant tidal estuary. Headwater streams flowing into these rivers pass through the site. Sustainable development principles agreed to in advance by community stakeholders guided the planning and design process. These principles called for a compact, walkable neighborhood with a diversity of dwelling types, a well-connected street network

Figure 3.7 Heritage Park: stormwater gardens where Bassett Creek once flowed.

Figure 3.8 East Clayton: Park and wetland adjacent to a restored stream. (Source: James Taylor Chair for Landscape and Livable Environments; drawing by William Wenk)

of narrow, treed, pedestrian-friendly streets with rear alleys for automobile storage and services, and the preservation of natural resources and natural drainage systems.

The 618-acre site will eventually be home to about 13,000 people. Under construction in 2005, the compact, mixed-use community will include a broad range of housing types, from rental apartments to both attached and detached single-family homes. A neighborhood commercial "main street" along the western edge of the community, mixed-use residential areas within the community, and a business park will provide services and jobs for residents. A finely grained, grid-based street network with alleys will provide high levels of connectivity for vehicles, pedestrians, and bicycles while also serving utility and environmental functions.

Protecting the headwater streams that flow into the Nikomekl and Serpentine rivers was a high priority for East Clayton. To that end, principle 7 read: "Preserve the natural environment and promote natural drainage systems." Designers used three primary strategies to fulfill this principle: (1) protecting and enhancing on-site stream and drainage corridors, (2) promoting a surface drainage system aimed at maintaining the site's predevelopment hydrology, and (3) limiting the amount of impervious surface in the development. The green network on the site knits together a system of "riparian" neighborhood and school parks with both naturally existing and constructed riparian corridors and stormwater wetlands. Even the street system is designed to contribute to environmental goals. These "green streets" will provide a secondary green network for the neighborhood (Figure 3.9). As designed, narrow, curbless pavement drains to adjacent infiltration swales, which are lined with generous tree-planting areas.[36] This diverse, finely scaled network of green infrastructure in the neighborhood performs environmental services that help protect the region's ecological structure.

Developed between 1991 and 1996 as a component of the Livable Region Strategic Plan, Vancouver's Green Zone is a regionally scaled vision of ecological structure that provided a context for the East Clayton sustainable development plan (Figure 3.10). In 1991, the metropolitan region around Vancouver, British Columbia, was projected to grow by 1 million people in thirty years. Currently, it is home to about 2 million people and is pro-

Figure 3.9 East Clayton: major streets and green network.

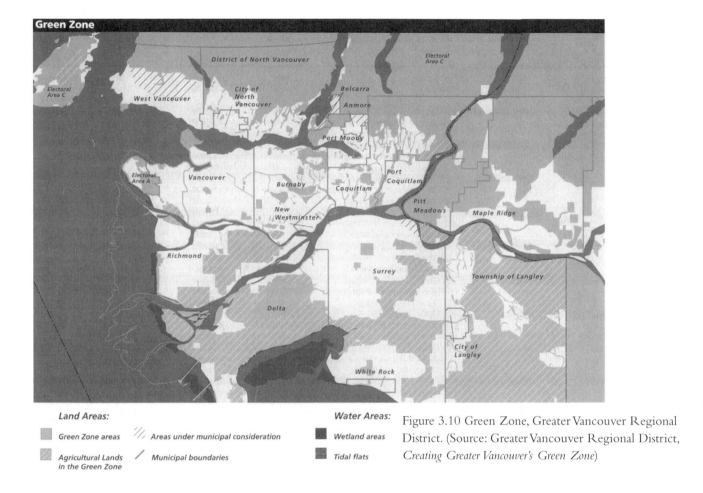

Green Zone

Land Areas:

Green Zone areas   Areas under municipal consideration

Agricultural Lands   Municipal boundaries
in the Green Zone

Water Areas:

Wetland areas

Tidal flats

Figure 3.10 Green Zone, Greater Vancouver Regional District. (Source: Greater Vancouver Regional District, *Creating Greater Vancouver's Green Zone*)

jected to grow to 4.8 million by 2100. The urbanized area already encompassed the full extent of land between the U.S. border and the mountain ranges that limit northern growth. With an ocean to the west, suburban expansion had nowhere to go but eastward along the Fraser River Valley, an area of prime agricultural land serving much of Canada and beyond. In a reversal of typical growth management planning, the Greater Vancouver Regional District (GVRD), the regional planning authority, began planning for an additional 1 million people in the landlocked lower mainland by first engaging the region to identify the Green Zone— "globally significant" natural resources that were in need of protection from urban development. The Green Zone includes community health lands, such as the city's watersheds located in the North Shore mountains and floodplains; ecologically important

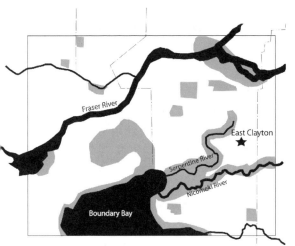

Figure 3.11 Green Zone, Delta Surrey detail, Greater Vancouver Regional District. (Source: derived from Greater Vancouver Regional District, *Creating Greater Vancouver's Green Zone*)

lands, including the forested mountain slopes, wetlands, and important ecological corridors; outdoor recreation and scenic lands, including parks and trails; and renewable resource lands, including agriculture and forestry lands (Figure 3.11). The Livable Region Strategic Plan, adopted by GVRD in 1994 and by all member municipalities by 1996, emphasizes four strategies: protecting the Green Zone, building complete communities, achieving compact development, and increasing transportation choices.[37]

Vancouver's Green Zone is a crude yet visionary sketch of the metropolitan region's ecological structure. Conceived in advance of regional growth management and transportation planning, it guides ecological planning efforts at many scales. The East Clayton neighborhood, a mere pixel on regional plans, responded directly to the Livable Region strategy and the Green Zone. Its finely scaled green network of streams, drainage ways, and wetlands will help preserve a healthy hydrology and provide small corridors for ecological connectivity while also serving multiple human purposes.

As discussed above, cross-scaled ecological planning is beginning to show results in Portland, Oregon, and Vancouver, British Columbia. In both cities, regional policies and plans have identified and prioritized protection of the region's green networks. The cities in each region have responded with plans of their own, for which they encourage or mandate compliance. In both cases, regional and city plans provide information and a framework for neighborhood-scale plans, such as Villebois and East Clayton. Neighborhood-scale networks may be primarily streets, bikeways, drainage corridors, or open space, yet they can contribute significantly to the functioning and health of the neighborhood when they serve multiple human and natural functions. Most important, by allowing natural processes to occur within and along these corridors and networks, the neighborhood's green networks can contribute to a healthy metropolitan ecosystem.

Green Networks Strategies

- Create a vision for protecting, restoring, and interconnecting the city's ecological structure.
- Identify and plan multifunctional green networks at every

planning scale: the metropolitan area, the city, and the neighborhood.

- Engage the research community and the citizenry to study the city's ecosystem and the elements of its ecological structure.
- Employ landscape restoration to repair the torn and fragmented fabric of the structure.
- Incorporate natural processes in the design of urban landscapes, and make these natural processes visible.

Chapter 4
Gray Networks

> Residents of the Northwest states use fully 57 percent more gasoline per person than their BC neighbors. British Columbia's lower consumption is a result of the province's more compact communities and smaller road network. . . . Compact cities with fewer roads yield less driving.
>
> Northwest Environment Watch, *Cascadia Scorecard*

Urban populations depend on the importing of massive quantities of food, water, energy, and goods and on the roughly analogous exporting of liquid and solid wastes. Networks of roads, sidewalks, and transit move people and goods into, around, and out of the city, while water, electricity, communications, and gas lines as well as stormwater and sanitary sewers distribute essential services. These systems are akin to the human body's circulatory, nervous, and digestive systems. The circulatory system would be the street, electricity, water, and gas systems; the nervous system would be the city's increasingly sophisticated communications networks; and the digestive system would include the stormwater, wastewater, and solid waste removal systems. In post–World War II North America, we have approached these systems as technical problems requiring technological fixes. Their design has been narrowly focused on utilitarian functions and divorced from natural processes and civic or aesthetic roles.

Since the late 1980s, environmental scientists have recognized that this narrow, functional approach to the design of roads, stormwater, and wastewater systems has human and environmental costs. In the case of streets and highways, standards set by the Institute of Transportation Engineers as early as 1942 have largely determined the design of all U.S. streets and highways, with a mandate of achieving the efficient, free, and rapid flow of traffic.[1] These traffic-oriented street designs have severely reduced people's opportunities to use nonpolluting modes of transportation, such as bicycling and walking. Coupled with widely dispersed land uses, vehicle-enabling road networks have contributed to exponential growth in vehicle miles traveled throughout North America and to vehicle-related air and water pollution. By the 1980s, streets, sewers, and other urban infrastructure had become serious urban environmental problems.

Urban circulation systems—streets, transit ways, bikeways, and pedestrian pathways—are what we call gray networks in this book (Figure 4.1). At the neighborhood scale, gray networks serve people's day-to-day needs of circulation while also playing other roles, from meeting and play spaces to locations for trash collection and emergency services. They commonly include associated utility corridors, which must be integrated into their design, but in this chapter we will focus on the layout and design of the circulatory networks themselves. As components of metropolitan transportation networks, neighborhood-scale networks must effectively connect to these larger systems but must also serve other purposes independently. The best neighborhood networks adequately serve travel, service, and emergency vehicles while also providing beautiful, safe places to play, walk, bike, ride, hang out, and garden.

Gray Networks Impact Pollution

> Every gallon of gasoline burned sends about 20 pounds carbon dioxide, containing 5 pounds of carbon, into the atmosphere. . . . It's like tossing a five-pound bag of charcoal briquettes out the window every 20 miles or so.
>
> J. Ryan, director, Northwest Environmental Watch

Because the design of streets dramatically influences whether people will walk or bike or must drive, gray networks affect air pollution. The form of the city's streets, in conjunction with land uses and transit access, also influences how much residents drive and for what purposes.[2] Travel patterns within and between urban areas contribute significantly to air pollution. Despite notable, extensive improvements in vehicle technology, automobiles remain a major source of air pollutants and, to a lesser extent, of greenhouse gases in metropolitan areas. The rate at which we acquire and use automobiles is growing faster than the population.

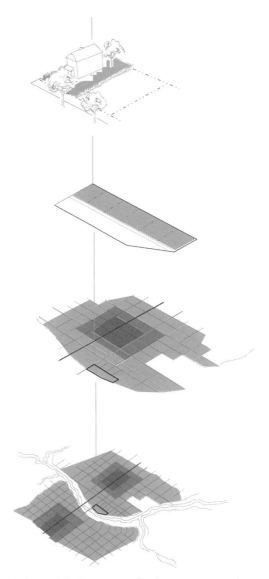

Figure 4.1 Gray networks shown across scales.

Between 1969 and 1995, while the U.S. population increased by 23 percent, the number of cars and the amount we use them increased much faster. We went from a society of roughly one car per household to one of roughly two per household. During that same period, the number of cars on the road and the number of vehicle miles traveled per year more than doubled.[3]

Where and how we use vehicles influence the type and quantity of emissions. The number of miles we travel, the number of trips we make, the speeds at which we travel, and the patterns by which we drive all have an impact on air quality. Carbon monoxide emissions, for example, are a product of incomplete combustion typically generated by any of a number of fuel-rich, congested urban driving situations, such as cold starts, travel at low speeds, rapid acceleration, and steep grades and declines as speeds approach 55 miles per hour. Nitrogen oxide emissions, on the other hand, increase with speed.[4] The number of trips, rather than the vehicle miles traveled, may become more important in controlling emissions. EPA researchers, for example, estimate that by 2010 more than half of emissions will be attributable to stops and starts rather than to miles traveled.[5]

In 1999, the average American household generated about 6.5 vehicle trips on an average day and about 21,000 vehicle miles traveled per year, up from 18,000 in 1990.[6] Both factors—the number of trips and the length of those trips—have economic and environmental impact and, in turn, can be positively or negatively affected by community planning and design. Development patterns that reduce vehicle use also reduce vehicle miles traveled, vehicle starts, and congestion, and they may encourage alternative modes of travel. All of these factors reduce the sources of pollution. According to the U.S. Department of Transportation: "Increased usage of bicycle and walking modes . . . replace[s] a motorized person trip with a non-motorized person trip. From the standpoint of traffic congestion and highway capacity, higher rates of bicycle and pedestrian usage should reduce vehicle trip demand and traffic congestion. . . . From the standpoint of air quality, . . . because the trips are relatively short, the primary benefit is in the elimination of vehicle trips ('cold start' emissions) over VMT."[7] In Greater Vancouver, British Columbia, where two-thirds of the population lives in compact neighborhoods, the typical car or truck travels 15 miles per day, whereas in Seattle, with only a quarter of the population living at compact densities, the typical car or truck travels 19 miles. Per capita gasoline consumption is also lower in British Columbia, at 5.5 gallons (20.9 liters) compared to Washington's 8.4 gallons (31.8 liters) per week.[8]

Designing Street Networks

How we plan and design neighborhood street networks and land use can be a part of the solution. Mixing places of work, shopping, education, and recreation within a compact neighborhood of at least 12 persons per acre potentially reduces demand for vehicle trips.[9] Bringing activities, such as homes and grocery store, closer together; finely mixing those that are mutually supportive; and connecting them in ways that attract pedestrian and bicycle travel can reduce vehicle-related emissions and improve air quality. Contemporary principles of street network design, such as those espoused by the new urbanism and smart growth movements, recommend diverse choices and comfortable, well-connected, safe environments for all modes of travel. Integrated networks that accommodate buses, cars, bicycles, and pedestrians in attractive street environments are believed to encourage more pedestrian travel.[10] Several recent studies have confirmed that in general, this pattern does that effectively.[11] In a study of twelve neighborhoods, University of Washington professor Anne Vernez Moudon found that in neighborhoods with relatively equal density and access by distance to neighborhood services, those with smaller block sizes and continuous, well-connected sidewalk systems had three times as many pedestrians as those with large blocks and inconsistent, discontinuous sidewalk systems.[12]

Accessibility and connectivity are two significant measures of network effectiveness. *Accessibility* refers to both normative and measurable physical qualities. Normative factors include attractiveness of destinations and the ease of getting there, while physical factors include how many and how easy the points of access and egress are and whether or not impediments occur. Greater physical or spatial accessibility means the ability to move safely and unimpeded from a starting point to a destination.[13] Good accessibility can increase the likelihood that potential travelers

will be able to use the network. Greater *connectivity,* the potential for choice and flexibility of movement, can reduce traffic volume and congestion on through streets and increase choice and
variety as travelers choose alternate paths to a common destination.
Connectivity is measured by comparing the number of intersection points to the number of "links" or lengths of pathway. Generally, the greater the number of access points and intersections,
the higher the connectivity of a network.[14] Lesser connectivity
typically directs more vehicles onto fewer streets, increasing traffic volume and congestion on connecting streets, which in turn
can create a hostile environment (of speed, noise, poor air quality,
and few crossing opportunities) for pedestrians and bicyclists.[15]

Using alternative modes of transportation, such as buses, bicycles, or walking, must seem quick, easy, and pleasant to potential users. Therefore, use of these modes directly relates to attractiveness, safety, accessibility, and connectivity.[16] After distance, the
next indicator of an effective pedestrian and bicycle network is
the presence of continuous, well-connected, safe, and physically
accessible sidewalks and bicycle paths.[17] Sidewalks and walking
paths, in particular, need to connect continuously to destinations,
preferably by the shortest distance.[18] For pedestrians, attractiveness is further related to the perceived safety and interest of the
experience. Pedestrian safety directly relates to adjacent traffic
speed, traffic volume, safe crossings, and having clearly delineated
places to walk and separation or buffering from traffic. Most fundamental for pedestrian safety is the presence of a sidewalk alongside streets. Perceptions of safety increase where physical buffers
exist, such as planting strips or lines of parked cars between the
street and the sidewalk.[19] Transportation planner Reid Ewing
proposes that sidewalks are needed along both sides of all arterial
and collector streets and along at least one side of low-volume
local streets (fewer than 250 trips per day).[20]

Bicycle safety is in large part associated with clearly delineated, on-street travel lanes or off-street paths. Cyclists range in
age from very young children to elderly persons; as such, they
range in ability and endurance as well. Trip types range from
recreational and play to purposeful commutes and from short
hops to long excursions. Bicycle networks are best when they include both on- and off-street, interconnected networks that provide cyclists with a choice of route suited to their purpose and

abilities. Communities that exhibit high rates of bicycle use, such as Corvallis, Oregon, have extensive, well-connected systems of both on- and off-street bicycle lanes or paths. Those communities with high rates of bicycle commuting to school have separate bike lanes and paths or designated low-volume streets.[21]

The two most common types of street networks found in the United States are the grid (traditional street networks) network and "loops and lollipops," the more hierarchical and curvilinear patterns common to suburban subdivisions.[22] Traditional grid networks, the standard street network of the late-nineteenth and early-twentieth centuries, are designed to have short block lengths, straight streets, and back alleys in every block (Figure 4.2). The alleys provide service and parking at the rear of buildings, allowing for narrower lots and higher densities of development (Figure 4.3). Whereas curvilinear street systems tend to be circuitous and poorly connected, thus discouraging walking, grid street systems provide more direct connections for pedestrians and automobiles. The fine grain of these networks also provides high levels of connectivity with many route choices. Access to the system is from multiple points, and travel is usually unimpeded; thus, accessibility is also high. With car storage and trash located along the alley, these streets tend to be more attractive for pedestrians. Because of greater accessibility and connectivity, the grid has become the network of choice for the new urbanist and smart growth movements.

Loop and lollipop systems are designed to limit vehicular traffic on residential streets by making as many loop roads or dead-end cul-de-sacs as possible. Collector streets pick up traffic from the small local streets and feed into arterial streets, the high-volume through streets. These networks are derived from the superblock design by Clarence Stein and Henry Wright for Radburn, New Jersey (see the case study in Chapter 2).[23] That plan was intended to create a residential environment that separated pedestrian and vehicular traffic with an internal park and walkways system and an external, or perimeter, roadway system (Figure 4.4). An off-street network of walkways, intended to protect children's safety, drove the network design. With the separated walkways, children could travel throughout the neighborhood to schools, parks, and playgrounds without crossing major streets. Houses were located in small groupings on cul-de-sacs, and all

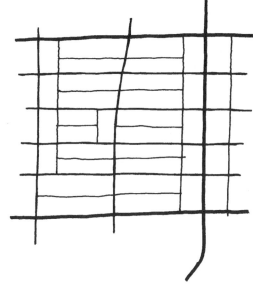

Figure 4.2 A typical grid-based street network.

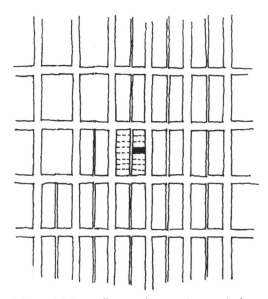

Figure 4.3 Lots, alleys, and streets in a typical grid-based neighborhood.

vehicular traffic was directed to perimeter roads around the so-called superblocks of houses, schools, and parks.[24] During the early post–World War II era, the U.S. Federal Housing Administration promoted a derivation of this scheme to help decrease the costs of infrastructure in residential areas. Unfortunately, the crucial pedestrian circulation system was often left out, leaving residential neighborhoods with loop and lollipop road systems but very poor connectivity, especially for pedestrians (Figure 4.5).[25]

Both of these common street network types have benefits and liabilities. Because cul-de-sacs have no through traffic, and thus have low traffic volumes, loop and lollipop systems are attractive to home buyers yet contribute to greater overall vehicle use.[26] Whereas gridiron street systems typically provide high levels of both connectivity and accessibility, they perform less well when evaluated for safety. Gridiron street systems have more four-way intersections (the site of many accidents) per total length of street and often have longer view corridors for drivers, allowing increased speeds. In a study of these networks and a third type with all homes on cul-de-sacs (sidewalks were present on at least one side of all streets), Ben-Joseph found that accident rates on the grid system were 55 percent greater than on the loop and lollipop system, and 400 percent higher than on the cul-de-sac system.[27] Southworth and Ben-Joseph reference a study done by Harold Marks in 1957, which found that curvilinear, limited-access residential street systems with many T intersections had one accident to every eight in a gridiron system.[28] Grid networks also affect urban water systems. Of the two network types described above, the grid patterns typically generate 20 to 25 percent more total street length and as much as 35 percent more impervious surface than the curvilinear patterns.[29] This is largely due to the small block size and the addition of alleys. As discussed in Chapter 7, total impervious surface is an important indicator of impact on local hydrology.

Hybrid Networks

Although cul-de-sacs are the preferred residential street type and place for lot location, they are less preferred as an overall neighborhood form. This might suggest a desire for a neighborhood pattern where

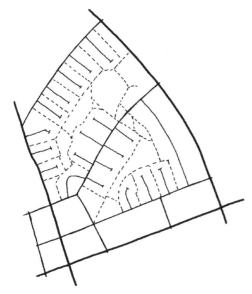

Figure 4.4 Radburn: diagram of the streets and pedestrian paths (dashed).

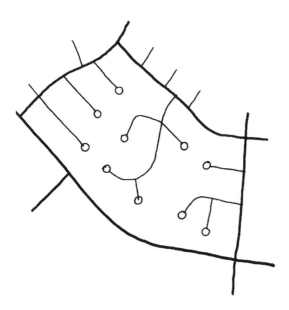

Figure 4.5 A typical loops and lollipops network.

residents attain the qualities associated with a dead-end street in their immediate surroundings, and the connective qualities associated with the grid in the larger context of their neighborhood.

E. Ben-Joseph, *Livability and Safety of Suburban Street Patterns*

Both grid and loop and lollipop network types have their advantages. Grids provide very good connectivity and accessibility and, with alleys, more vehicular storage and expanses of driveways away from the primary pedestrian area. Loops and lollipops maximize residents' safety because many of the homes are on short streets with very low traffic volumes. These systems typically have less overall street area, even with wider streets. A hybrid network—one that favors the pedestrian and bicyclist while still providing a well-connected vehicular network, thus incorporating the best of both systems—may be the next wave of experimentation.[30] Since vehicles move about eight times faster than pedestrians through residential areas, a well-connected street system can include longer distances for vehicles than for pedestrians and bicycles.

The modified grid, in which some cross streets are replaced with paths for pedestrians and bicycles, is an obvious option (Figure 4.6). Larger vehicular blocks with more finely scaled pedestrian connections would immediately reduce impervious surfaces because of fewer cross streets. Pedestrian or midblock paths enhance a neighborhood's pedestrian and cycling network by providing off-street choices for pedestrians. These paths are not only narrower but can also be paved with pervious surfaces, thus reducing impervious surface area. The Beach in Toronto (see the case study in Chapter 2) demonstrates such a hybrid street network. Long vehicular blocks stretch from Queen Street toward the beach, creating distant vistas to Lake Ontario along each street corridor. Midway down the 875-foot-long streets, an east-west pedestrian path skirts between houses, connecting all residents to a large new park at the neighborhood's western border (Figure 4.7).

Revisiting the principles of the Radburn network (see the case study in Chapter 2) provides another model for hybrid networks. Circulation networks that separate primary vehicular traffic from a pedestrian and bicycle system remain a valid model for residential areas. With these systems, houses are served on one side by vehicular access and on the other by pedestrian access. Homes have

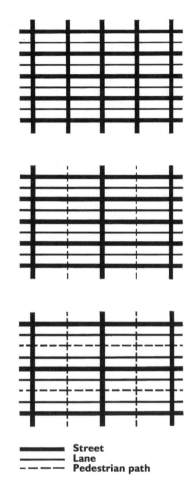

Street
Lane
Pedestrian path

Figure 4.6 A typical grid-based street network (top) and two derivations. In the middle diagram, alternating cross streets are replaced with pedestrian paths; in the bottom diagram, alternating streets in both directions are replaced with pedestrian paths.

Figure 4.7 The Beach: midblock pedestrian path linking the neighborhood to the park.

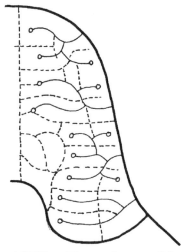

Figure 4.8 Village Homes: diagram of the streets and pedestrian paths (dashed).

Figure 4.9 Northwest Landing: a cluster of homes front onto open space.

two fronts rather than the clear front and back yards of conventional development. Village Homes in Davis, California, uses a modification of the Radburn street system. A finely scaled grid of off-street paths interconnects all areas of the neighborhood (Figure 4.8). Vehicles use a street system of cul-de-sacs served by an adjacent collector street. These low-volume residential streets weave through the interconnected system of green spaces used for circulation, stormwater drainage, and agriculture. At Village Homes, carports and private walled gardens abut narrow residential streets, whereas the more public side of each house is on the greenway.[31]

Hybrid networks also help to work around environmental assets and with difficult topography. Along streams or wetlands, where frequent crossings would harm natural systems, cul-de-sacs may be used to break the vehicular grid. Pedestrian connectivity, however, can be retained using paths, bridges, and boardwalks between cul-de-sac ends and along interior greenways without significantly increasing imperviousness. In difficult topography, streets should follow contours to reduce disturbing the ground. Cross streets that might fall on steep grades can be replaced with pedestrian paths. In select cases, alleys may suffice for vehicular connections to homes, allowing front streets to be replaced with green space. An example of this use of alleys occurs at Northwest Landing in Washington. In this case, a common green, which allowed a cluster of mature trees to be protected, serves as the front of the homes (Figure 4.9). Vehicular access to the homes is from a rear alley for residents, while visitor parking is provided on a nearby side street. A street network like this is also planned for Southeast False Creek in Vancouver, home of the Olympic Village in 2010 (see Chapter 8).

Green Streets

Local-scale gray networks represent 20 to 30 percent of the land area of most neighborhoods.[32] Such networks require a significant investment both in land area and in capital and operating tax dollars for most jurisdictions. Because gray networks are paved, they also contribute to water pollution. Impervious surface is land covered by roads, rooftops, parking lots, driveways, sidewalks, patios, and any other surface that prevents water penetration into the soil. When land is covered with these surfaces, rainwater cannot follow its natural drainage cycles. Instead, precipitation runs off rooftops, over paved surfaces, along street gutters, and eventually into the stormwater system. Impervious surfaces generate far more runoff than natural areas because none of it is stored or infiltrates into the ground. Runoff generated from an undeveloped watershed can increase by about 500 percent once the area is developed.[33] The street system typically represents more than half of a residential area's total impervious surface coverage and, thus, contributes significantly to urban runoff.[34]

A direct correlation exists between urban runoff volumes and amounts of stormwater pollution. Pollutants, such as oil, grease, and metals coming from automobiles and phosphorus and nitrogen coming from fertilizer and natural decomposition, accumulate on impervious surfaces between rainstorms. Rainfall then washes these pollutants along streets, into the stormwater system, and into natural waterways. Because most urban stormwater is untreated, high percentages of impervious surfaces yield high rates of runoff and equally high rates of stormwater-related pollution. Since street paving represents such a significant portion of impervious surfaces, planning and design strategies that reduce the total area of streets can be crucial to environmental protection. Reducing the extent of street networks, decreasing street widths, using pervious pavements, and reducing the amount of paved parking coverage all help to decrease the quantity and effects of impervious surfaces.

The term "green streets" has recently been adopted by many cities to refer to streets that emphasize environmental quality in numerous ways, including reducing pavement widths, increasing tree planting, and incorporating stormwater treatment. Seattle's land use code, for example, codified green streets in 1993, defining them as "a street right-of-way which is part of the street circulation pattern, that through a variety of treatments, such as sidewalk widening, landscaping, traffic calming, and pedestrian-oriented features is enhanced for pedestrian circulation and open space use."[35] Specific streets have been mapped as green streets, and the code requires that these streets be renovated to the new standards when significant new development occurs. Although named green streets, however, they are seldom required to include stormwater treatment, especially in the central city areas. A more aggressive planning-oriented program exists in Portland, Oregon. Portland's regional planning authority, known as Metro, published a green streets guidebook in 2000 to encourage cities, designers, and developers in its jurisdiction to include stormwater mitigation and habitat protection as integral aspects of street design. The guidebook, which was distributed to all regional agencies and sold nationwide, explained why and how to design streets that would have much lower impacts on natural water resources. In Portland, green streets are intended to treat and reduce runoff by incorporating stormwater detention and treatment in the street right-of-way. They are also designed to reduce the negative impacts of overall street networks on streams and associated habitat. The guidebook proposes reducing the total number of stream crossings and using bridges whenever possible.[36]

Portland's green streets guidebook documented the negative impacts of multiple stream crossings on fish and other riparian and aquatic populations. It also provided guidance about how to design stream-sensitive street networks. The booklet demonstrates that in contemporary smart growth neighborhoods, local streets are designed into a grid of approximately 250 feet by 400 feet. Along 1 mile of stream corridor, if all streets were to cross the stream, there could be thirteen to twenty-one culverted stream crossings. Each such crossing affects habitat values for both fish and terrestrial species and can cause changes to stream structure. Green street networks protect natural resources by aligning streets with topography and natural features, reducing the frequency of crossings, and designing low-impact crossings such as bridges. Full vehicular crossings may be replaced periodically with pedestrian and bicycle bridges. Additional efforts to reduce total impervious surfaces associated with streets, and to treat stormwater alongside roads, further reduces the impacts on the watershed.[37]

The Royal Avenue Plan in Eugene, Oregon, exemplifies the green streets approach (also see Chapter 1). The plan was designed according to new urbanist principles of a fine-grained gridiron street plan with mixed uses in a compact form. The building block for the street system was a 250- by 400-foot block with a rear alley and two intersecting, centrally located collector streets linking this neighborhood to adjacent areas. Imperatives of wetland protection caused the plan to be incrementally reshaped to protect the wetlands and to integrate open stormwater drainage. In refining the plan, the grid-based street network was skewed around three armatures of drainage ways and wetlands (Figure 4.10). Important connecting streets, such as a neighborhood loop road, cross the greenways, but many local streets end for automobiles while continuing over bridges for pedestrians and bicycles (Figure 4.11). With one exception, stream crossings occur no closer than 350 feet and are as much as 800 feet apart. The plan also proposes stormwater filtration along the streets. On many streets, stormwater runoff will be directed to biofiltration swales located in center medians or street-side planting strips. With these measures in place, the streets themselves and their additive effects as a system will have far less impact on the development's newly restored greenways.

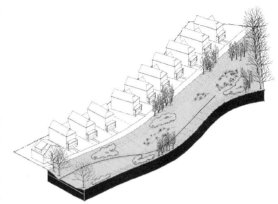

Figure 4.10 Royal Avenue: schematic design for the multi-use greenway.

Skinny Streets

Residential street standards dating back to the 1960s typically called for a 50- to 60-foot right-of-way with 34 to 36 feet of pavement. Millions of miles of residential streets in North America were built to these standards.[38] However, not only do these streets use a lot of land and add excessive amounts of impervious surfaces, but they also encourage unsafe speeds.[39] In recent years, these problems have been confirmed by national street standards associations that have recommended that residential streets be as narrow as 22 feet wide if they serve neighborhoods that produce low traffic volumes (fewer than fifty homes or five hundred daily trips).[40] Cities across the United States and Canada are now reevaluating their street design standards. Starting in 1991, Oregon's administrative rules required cities to review street design standards with a goal of reducing residential street widths, and by 2000 more than twenty cities and counties had adopted narrow street standards. In Portland, the city created a Skinny Street program, which has reduced minimum residential street widths by as much as 12 feet to 20 to 26 feet, depending on parking needs.[41] Although many people initially assume that narrower streets are unsafe, the opposite is true in many cases. Safety has been correlated with narrower residential street widths. In a study of the relationship between physical characteristics of streets and accidents, a high correlation was found between street width and

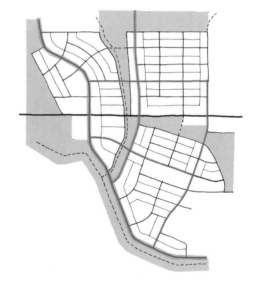

Figure 4.11 Royal Avenue: diagram of the streets and pedestrian paths (dashed) with greenways shown in gray.

accidents. A typical 36-foot-wide residential street had 1.21 collisions per mile per year, whereas a 24-foot-wide street had 0.32 collisions per mile per year.[42]

A version of a skinny street that effectively reduces both pavement widths and travel speeds is called a queuing street. With this type, one shared travel lane of about 14 feet in width serves traffic flowing in both directions. One of two oncoming vehicles must pull into the parking lane to allow the other to pass.[43] Although intuition suggests otherwise, practice in numerous cities has demonstrated that any inconvenience caused by the lack of two moving lanes is remarkably low in single-family areas.[44] The very narrow profile of the street, as well as the need to be on the lookout for oncoming traffic, forces reduced speeds, which in turn increase pedestrian and bicycle safety. Queuing streets are the norm in the densely populated Kitsilano neighborhood (pictured in Figure 4.12) as well as in many other neighborhoods in Vancouver, British Columbia. It is also the contemporary standard used in Portland and other Oregon cities for low-volume residential streets. Traffic is forced to move slowly, while parking buffers pedestrians; as a result, the street is very pedestrian friendly.

Modest reductions in the dimension of streets, sidewalks, and rights-of-way may appear insignificant in streetscape designs from block to block. However, when compounded at a larger scale, these changes can significantly reduce impervious surface, stormwater runoff, and stormwater pollution while enhancing the overall character of a neighborhood. In a 1995 study, Tom Schueler and colleagues estimated that it was possible to reduce impervious surface areas by 28 percent using a skinny street design with a 26-foot pavement width versus a traditional 36-foot street.[45] Narrower streets also conserve land, contributing to overall land use efficiencies; with less paved area, they also cost less to install and maintain. Skinny streets also have a more intimate scale, especially when lined with street trees. This attractiveness contributes to neighborhood livability.

Streets as Civic Amenity

The term "infrastructure" refers to the foundations for a system and is often used to collectively reference the gray networks ser-

Figure 4.12 A queuing street in the Kitsilano neighborhood of Vancouver, British Columbia.

vicing a city, including the transportation, communications, power, water, and sewer systems. The term, from the Latin *infra,* meaning "below" or "under," suggests that they are the inner (or hidden) structures of the city. The twentieth-century assumption that these urban systems were to be hidden and thus unknown is a relatively recent phenomenon. Until the mid-1900s, the builders of public works understood that prominent roads, bridges, and waterworks, as the most visible elements of public works, should be great civic works as well. Examples of beautiful works of infrastructure occur throughout North America, including nineteenth-century parkways, boulevards of the City Beautiful movements, streets of historic districts, and numerous roads and bridges built by the Work Projects Administration and the Civilian Conservation Corps in the United States during the depression era. But in North America, most urban development has occurred since World War II, in the modern design era. Functionalism, coupled with the very rapid pace of urbanization after the war, led to almost five decades' worth of infrastructure developed with little civic merit. The roads, water service, electricity, communications, gas, stormwater, and sanitary sewers of North American cities have been mostly utilitarian and intended for a single purpose. Many a once-beautiful neighborhood has been blighted by such constructions.

A renewed understanding of the civic role of public works emerged in the late twentieth century as city planners, urban designers, developers, and engineers began to understand the economic and social advantages of beautiful, pedestrian-friendly streets. Park planners, environmentalists, and engineers began to grasp that the open spaces of cities can serve many beneficial functions while getting the populations closer to nature. This idea that public works can serve civic functions has become a topic of lively debate among designers. In his 1996 article "Infrastructure as Landscape," Gary Strang argued that the inner workings of the city can and should be exposed and explained to urban people. Infrastructure—so crucial to the city's effective functioning—also deserves to be expressed in the landscape for ecological, educational, and artistic reasons.[46] The June 1995 issue of *Landscape Architecture* similarly called for a new attitude and attention toward works of urban infrastructure: "It is better that we accept technical infrastructure as the reality of human nature. In doing so, we may shape our landscapes to accommodate, express and control technology. In addition, we may use them to manifest the sustainable potentials and limitations of our communities and bioregions."[47] Projects in almost every major North American city exemplify this shift in attitude. For example, San Francisco removed the Embarcadero freeway after it was damaged in the 1989 earthquake and replaced it with a new pedestrian-friendly promenade (Figure 4.13).[48] Boston undertook the massive "Big Dig" project to bury its harbor-front freeway and cover it with parks and a more human-scale surface road.[49] Seattle and San Francisco have renovated sewage treatment plants to include interpretation, recreation, natural habitat, and beautiful landscaping.[50]

The intensity and complexity of modern cities mandate that we move beyond a narrow, functional, single-purpose infrastructure. Streets should be beautiful public spaces with rich pedestrian zones. Drainage corridors could be attractive water-quality facilities and corridors for people and wildlife. Highways could provide recreational and ecological corridors, and sewage treatment plants can be parks, as projects in Seattle and San Francisco demonstrate. At its highest level, urban infrastructure "operates as both a functioning system *and* poetic idea."[51] Because they are the most extensive of the city's public spaces, streets are the city's most important civic places, and they are once again gaining the attention of urban planners and designers. The new urbanists, who have heavily influenced all urban design since the mid-1990s, have strongly emphasized the design of streets, particularly to provide positive pedestrian spaces. As one designer observes: "The best streets create and leave strong, lasting impressions; they catch the eyes and the imagination."[52]

Heritage Park in Minneapolis and Stapleton in Denver are developments that created streets as important civic amenities (see the case studies in Chapter 2). Van White Memorial Boulevard at Heritage Park connects two halves of this redeveloped neighborhood that are separated by the multilane Olson Memorial Highway. The meandering boulevard pays tribute to Bassett Creek, which was buried and built over in the early 1900s. The new boulevard straddles a broad greenway with a re-created stream corridor interwoven with stormwater gardens (Figure 4.14). It connects two new parks and provides a focus for community ac-

Figure 4.13 The Embarcadero in San Francisco, California, after redevelopment.

tivities.[53] This street-cum-park-cum-water treatment facility clearly will be a social center and source of civic pride.

A similar gesture to site heritage was made by the planners of Stapleton, who aligned three avenues of the first and second neighborhoods with Stapleton Airport's former east-west runways and taxiways. Twenty-Ninth Avenue, a broad boulevard connecting Founder's Green on the west to the Westerly Creek Greenway on the east, has a promenade and park between two streets and will include seating and play areas (Figure 4.15). Founder's Green at the west will be a manicured park with a large community amphitheatre. Parks at the eastern end in the Westerly Creek Greenway will include active recreation facilities and natural areas along the creek.[54] Twenty-Ninth Avenue is the first of many boulevards that will structure this major new community in Denver.[55] Intended to connect visually and spatially to the surrounding city, these boulevards will be new additions to Denver's rich assemblage of grand streets and parkways. They will be beautiful, multipurpose amenities, elevating infrastructure to a higher civic role.

As Heritage Park, Stapleton, Royal Avenue, and Village Homes demonstrate, gray networks hold great potential to serve a complex set of infrastructure functions while also providing aesthetic and ecological services. One-size-fits-all street systems cannot serve diverse, complex, compact neighborhoods. Rather, neighborhoods need well-connected, multidimensional networks with purposefully designed streets and paths—some to emphasize vehicular movement, some to cater to pedestrians and bicycles, some to avoid natural resources, some to clean and store stormwater, many to do all of these, and a few to be grand and beautiful gestures. Gray networks need not be universally "gray"; rather, they hold the promise to be diverse, complex, and green.

Gray Networks Strategies

- Design street networks that provide a choice of route and good connectivity for vehicles.
- Provide the highest levels of accessibility and connectivity for pedestrians and bicycles.

Figure 4.14 Heritage Park: stormwater gardens and pedestrian paths flow down the middle of Van White Memorial Boulevard.

Figure 4.15 Stapleton: a linear park occupies the middle of Twenty-Ninth Avenue.

- Create beautiful, high-quality pedestrian and bicycle envi-ronments.
- Adapt street networks to fit site conditions and to avoid sen-sitive natural resources.
- Design green streets that manage their own stormwater and maximize tree canopy cover.
- Reduce total impervious surfaces of street systems by reduc-ing the overall lengths and widths of vehicular streets.
- Treat gray networks as significant contributors to civic amenity; make all streets and paths beautiful.

Chapter 5
Gray Fabric

fab·ric \ `fa-brik \ *noun* . . . the arrangement of physical components
in relation to each other

Merriam-Webster Online, http://www.m-w.com (2004)

Just as neighborhoods are the building blocks of cities, individual lots are the building blocks of neighborhoods (Figure 5.1). These lots, accumulated into city blocks where people live and work, create the urban fabric. This fabric is composed of shops, services, and offices (commercial uses); schools, community centers, and government offices (civic uses); warehousing and factories (industrial uses); a broad range of housing types; and parks and open spaces. Urban fabric lies between the green and gray networks and is connected by them. Because it is fully integrated with the green and gray networks in a city, it should always be planned as a part of the whole system. This chapter focuses on the built-up, gray urban fabric, while the next chapter considers the green urban fabric.

Sprawl, with its roughly two-to-one ratio between land consumption and population growth, has become the norm in North American cities, largely because of low-density development patterns (Figure 5.2). These widely dispersed and disaggregated land uses are connected by automobile-friendly but pedestrian-unfriendly networks. Two building patterns predominate in these landscapes: ever-larger single-family homes on individual plots of land and what are commonly called "big box" commercial services, which are large, single-purpose retail outlets sitting in the midst of very large surface parking lots. These low-density, sprawling development patterns have high environmental impacts while concurrently degrading people's health and quality of life. These impacts are clearly demonstrated in terms of their ecological footprints, or impacts on regional and global resources. An average working resident of Vancouver, British Columbia, living in an average suburban, single-family home and driving about 300 miles per week has an ecological footprint of 11 hectares

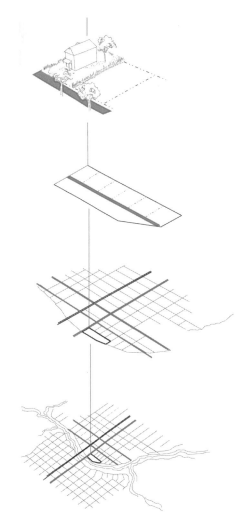

Figure 5.1 Gray fabric shown across scales from the yard to the city.

Figure 5.2 Bird's-eye view of typical low-density suburban development.

(27.2 acres). If that same person lived in a smaller, attached home closer to work, substituted some trips each week with walking or transit, and reduced driving to about 185 miles per week, he or she would reduce this ecological footprint to 6 hectares (14.8 acres)—clearly an improvement but still not globally sustainable. At the conclusion of their ecological footprint quiz, Redefining Progress states, "Worldwide there exists 1.8 biologically productive global hectares [of land] (4.4 acres) per person."[1]

The alternative to sprawl is more-compact neighborhood development. Compact development features higher densities; appropriate mixes of land uses (which include employment); a diversity of housing types, sizes, and costs; well-designed circulation networks that prioritize pedestrian and bicycle routes; and parks and open spaces located within walking distance of homes. Contemporary urban design theory suggests that neighborhoods can meet the demand for weekly shopping, recreation, and school trips, and this is particularly so when shopping and services are in close proximity, with easy pedestrian and bicycle access for many neighborhood households.[2] Numerous studies generally agree that these patterns not only consume less land but also can be associated with less automobile travel and therefore less air pollution.[3] Denser communities tend to produce fewer vehicle miles traveled (VMT) per capita. One particular study found that, for a similar set of activities, 1 mile of transit travel in a dense urban area replaces 4 to 8 miles of automobile travel in lower-density suburbs.[4] Others have found that land use patterns that integrate higher-density housing with commercial services and employment and also develop high-quality transit, bicycle, and pedestrian routes can reduce vehicle use.[5] Robert Cervero and Carolyn Radisch found that residents of a traditional streetcar suburb made 28 percent of their nonwork trips by foot as compared to 6 percent by residents of an automobile-oriented development.[6] Others found that the relationship of density to nonmotorized travel choices was nonlinear, with higher densities resulting in even higher rates of pedestrians and bicycles.[7] Planning and design standards are beginning to reflect this linkage. The Institute of Transportation Engineers allows vehicle trip rate reduction factors of 2 to 7 percent in sufficiently dense, mixed-use areas with good pedestrian and bicycle networks, and up to 20 percent when those areas are also served by transit and light rail.[8]

Northwest Environment Watch has compared patterns of growth in northwestern cities using census data and satellite imagery to demonstrate that development pattern and density matter more than raw population growth numbers.[9] For example, between 1986 and 2001, the greater Vancouver area population grew at an average annual rate of 2.6 percent, from 1.4 to just over 2 million. Over roughly the same period (1990–2000), the greater Seattle-Tacoma area population grew by about the same number of people but less quickly, at an average annual rate of 1.7 percent, from 2.5 million to just under 3 million. Because the Vancouver area encouraged compact development patterns more aggressively than did Seattle, the consequences of roughly similar rates of population growth have differed significantly.

Over this period, the proportion of population in the Vancouver area's compact neighborhoods (greater than 12 persons per acre) increased from 46 percent to 62 percent; the proportion in the densest, pedestrian-oriented neighborhoods almost doubled, from 6 to 11 percent. At the same time, the proportion of people living in car-dependent neighborhoods (fewer than 12 persons per acre) shrank. The Seattle-Tacoma area, on the other hand, has directed less population growth into compact neighborhoods—about 25 percent, or less than half of the Vancouver proportion. The consequence overall is that the developed Seattle area consumes about 75 percent more land per resident than does the developed Vancouver area.

A related comparison of growth patterns in two neighboring areas of Portland, Oregon, tells this story more vividly. The greater Portland area straddles the Columbia River, two states (Oregon and Washington), and four counties (Multnomah, Washington, and Clackamas in Oregon, and Clark in Washington). This area of approximately 1.4 million people (in 1990) grew steadily and rapidly, by an annual rate of 2.4 percent, roughly double the national average throughout the 1990s. That growth rate translates into a population increase of about 100 new residents a day and a total increase of 376,000 new residents by 2000. About 70 percent of these new residents chose to locate in suburban areas of the three Oregon counties. The remainder chose Clark County, in Washington.

This growth precipitated a loss of about 8 acres of farmland and open space per day in the region. However, because Oregon and Washington manage growth differently, the loss was not uniformly distributed. In general, Oregon has encouraged growth in more-compact developments through a combination of state and local laws, policies, plans, and programs than has Washington. Not surprisingly then, over that same period, the number of people living in compact neighborhoods (12 or more people per acre) in the Oregon counties increased to just over half the total population increase. On the Washington side, population in low-density development patterns (less than 1 to less than 12 people per acre) increased to just under three-quarters of total population growth and required conversion of about 40 percent more land from rural to suburban uses than did the Oregon counties. Had the population choosing the Oregon counties been accommodated in development patterns more like those in Washington, an additional 14 square miles of farmland and open space would have been lost to development.

Compact Neighborhoods

Compactness is a precondition for conserving land and encouraging people to get out of their cars.[10] Done in concert with an appropriate mix and intensity of land uses, and with strategically planned and designed green and gray networks, compactness is also a precondition for reducing pavement, automobile trips, energy consumption, and emissions of air pollutants per household. In urban development, the designation "compact" translates to buildings that are tightly grouped and multistoried. Commercial areas are compact when they are composed of multistoried buildings that include a variety of uses (Figures 5.3 and 5.4). For example, a building might have parking underground, retail on the ground floor, offices and restaurants above, and apartments above that. Compact forms of residential development are attached homes, with the smallest and most compact being stacked apartments and the least compact being attached, single-family homes, such as row houses. However, even row houses are three to five times as compact as most single-family homes.

Compactness is a relative measure. What is considered compact in a large city like Vancouver, British Columbia, will vary from what is compact in a small, sprawling city like Boise, Idaho.

Figure 5.3 Lowry: a low-density, auto-oriented shopping area.

Figure 5.4 Cornell: a mixed-use neighborhood shopping area.

In greater Vancouver, two-thirds of the population lives in neighborhoods that exceed 12 people per acre, whereas in Boise, only 7 percent of the population (in 2000) lived at those densities and most lived in neighborhoods with densities of between 1 and 5 persons per acre.[11] What is considered compact in downtown areas varies from what is compact in the suburbs. Vancouver's downtown West End neighborhood, composed primarily of apartment towers, had a 2001 population density of 84 persons per acre, or 55 dwellings per gross acre. However, in Vancouver's suburban area of Maple Ridge, residential densities of approximately 30 persons per acre in its new town center will be considered compact. Even North America's most compact urban areas pale in comparison to many European cities, suggesting that we still have much room for improvement. Our most compact cities, such as New York (8 persons/acre), Boston (5 persons/acre), and the city of Vancouver (9 persons/acre) equal, at best, half the density of such European cities as Amsterdam (20 persons/acre) and London (17 persons/acre).[12]

Density

> Density . . . is always a fundamental decision in city design. It sets the framework for all the other features and has far-reaching implications.
>
> K. Lynch, *A Theory of Good City Form*

Common measures of compactness include density and floor-area ratios. Density, the most common measure for residential areas, is the ratio between the numbers of dwellings or persons and the area of land. It is typically measured either by numbers of dwellings per acre (or hectare) or numbers of people per acre (or hectare). "Gross density," often used to measure the density of large areas, includes the entire area of land, including all land uses (not just dwellings), streets, and open spaces, whereas "net density" typically considers only the land dedicated to residential uses.[13] Floor-area ratio (or floor-space ratio), which compares the developed building floor area to the site area, is more commonly used for commercial and mixed-use areas occupied by multistory buildings.

In North America, very-low-density development includes areas with between 1 and 5 persons per acre. Low-density development includes areas with between 5 and 11 people per acre (approximately 3 to 5 dwellings per net acre), whereas development is considered compact when densities exceed 12 persons per acre (more than 6 dwellings per net acre).[14] Shopping areas with low-density, sprawling development patterns will have floor areas that are far less than the site area (e.g., a ratio of .25 to 1), whereas in compact neighborhood centers, floor area ratios will be at least 1.5 to 1. When net residential densities begin to exceed 10 dwellings per acre, a critical mass of people resides within a reasonable walking distance to support pedestrian-oriented commercial services, viable transportation services, parks, and schools.[15] Planner Eliot Allen recommends that average densities in new urbanist developments should be in the range of 15 to 30 dwellings per net acre, roughly four times higher than conventional, low-density developments.[16]

Not surprisingly, compactness depends on the size and arrangement of residential buildings, on their relationship to one another and to the land. In North America, the most common residential building types include single-family, detached homes on individual lots; various types of low-rise, attached, single-family housing; stacked, walk-up apartments; and high-rise towers. The highest densities—and thus greatest compactness—are typically achieved in neighborhoods populated by high-rise buildings. However, in North America, high-rise housing is considered most suitable for nonfamily households, whereas families and large households are considered better housed in larger dwellings with good access to yards, playgrounds, and gardens.[17]

Many ground-oriented, low-rise forms of housing—such as stacked townhouses, row houses, triplexes, and duplexes—can meet thresholds for compact neighborhoods while also providing such amenities as ground-related entries, private or semiprivate yards, parking nearby, and opportunities to personalize the home and yard. For example, the historic Kitsilano neighborhood in Vancouver, British Columbia, once a neighborhood of large, single-family homes, is now a neighborhood containing a full array of low-rise housing with walk-up apartments, many derivations of attached homes (such as row houses and duplexes), and single-family, detached houses with apartments (Figures 5.5 and

Figure 5.5 Aerial photograph of the Kitsilano neighborhood in Vancouver, British Columbia. Each grid cell equals 1 acre.

5.6). Single-family, detached housing with ground-level apartments is common throughout the neighborhood (as well as in much of Vancouver) (Figure 5.7). Such structures double the residential density and concurrently provide affordable rental housing in desirable neighborhoods. This very walkable, family-oriented neighborhood has a density of almost 30 persons per acre, or 16 dwellings per gross acre.[18]

Entire neighborhoods do not need to have the same density; in fact, to achieve housing diversity, densities and types of housing must be varied. "Graded density" refers to the concept of clustering the highest density at and around a mixed-use service center while gradually decreasing residential densities toward the farthest reaches of the neighborhood.[19] This strategy maximizes the population near the center while achieving an average density that will support pedestrian-oriented neighborhood services and also provide a range of choices in housing types and costs. For example, to achieve an average net density of about 9 dwellings per acre, detached and attached single-family and multifamily buildings, ranging from about 6 to 20 dwellings per acre of land, can be mixed. Density gradients were proposed by architect Peter Calthorpe for Sacramento County's transit-oriented developments (TOD) in the late 1980s and referred to as primary and secondary residential areas. Calthorpe's concept was to include higher-density housing in the primary residential area, closest to the transit station at the neighborhood center. At Laguna West, a TOD started in 1990, housing in the neighborhood center area was to be restricted to walk-up apartments and attached, single-family housing. The lowest-density single-family, detached housing was restricted to the outer perimeter of the development, while the middle distance included a mix of attached and detached homes on small lots. Thus, the smallest proportion of the population would be beyond the walkable range.[20]

A similar approach to dispersing and averaging density occurs in new urbanist developments throughout the United States and Canada. Such developments often average 15 to 30 dwellings per acre, using a range of dwelling types and densities. Near town centers, densities range from 20 to 75 dwellings per acre and can be as high as 50 to 100 units per acre in more centrally located communities. Away from the town centers, net densities range from 6 to 25 units per acre.[21]

Figure 5.6 Kitsilano in Vancouver: a multifamily dwelling with four owner-occupied apartments.

Figure 5.7 Kitsilano in Vancouver: a single-family home with two ground-level rental apartments.

Complete Neighborhoods

The "completeness" of a neighborhood refers to the extent to which daily and weekly needs are close to homes. Mixing places of work, shopping, education, and recreation within a compact neighborhood potentially reduces demand for vehicle trips. Bringing those activities that are interdependent closer together, finely mixing those that are mutually supportive (where appropriate), and connecting all such activities in ways that attract pedestrian and bicycle travel can reduce vehicle use and related emissions and thus improve air quality.

Completeness transcends scales. Within any major metropolitan area, each municipality comprises a number of neighborhoods. Ideally, complete communities will exist at several scales so that the opportunity exists to live close to work. "Complete communities" is a term adopted by the Greater Vancouver Regional District (GVRD) to encapsulate a key principle of that region's growth management planning. The GVRD plan identifies eight high-density regional centers along existing or planned light rail lines and many smaller district centers. These so-called town centers each serve as the downtown for municipalities whose populations range from 1,500 to 400,000 (excluding the city of Vancouver). The regional growth plan emphasizes that these centers should be complete, meaning that they should include a balance of jobs that are close to where people live and accessible by transit; shops and services near homes; and a wide choice of housing types within and around each center.[22]

The smallest scale of this continuum is the neighborhood, which should also be complete. Complete neighborhoods need to provide day-to-day and week-to-week services, such as grocery stores, banks, medical facilities, coffee shops, restaurants, hair salons, day-care centers, schools, and parks (Figure 5.8). Although a balance of jobs will not likely exist in every neighborhood, each neighborhood can provide some working space and an appropriately sized commercial and service center in the heart of the neighborhood. Compatible civic uses (schools and churches) and recreational uses (parks and squares) should be nearby. For local stores and services to thrive, potential customers must close enough to sustain them economically. Industry standards propose a minimum of 1,500 households (3,000 to 3,500 people) to sup-

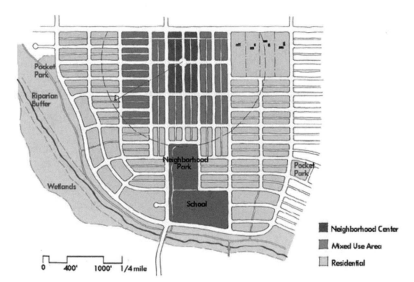

Figure 5.8 Prototype drawing for a complete, compact neighborhood.

Neighborhood Center
Mixed Use Area
Residential

port neighborhood commercial establishments.[23] However, Calthorpe suggests that it takes 10,000 people, or 2 square miles of mixed-density development, to support a full-service grocery store.[24] In terms of how much land is needed for a commercial center, Lynch suggests one-half to two-thirds of an acre (about 20,000 to 30,000 square feet) of local neighborhood commercial space per 1,000 inhabitants.[25]

Recent concepts of neighborhood composition, organization, and design bear similarities. For example, they typically cluster commercial and mixed-use areas at a neighborhood center located close to a major arterial roadway or a transit line (or both). Around the mixed-use center are higher-density residential areas—often stacked townhouses or walk-up apartments. Beyond that, housing densities gradually decrease from row housing to small-lot, single-family homes to larger-lot, single-family homes. Contemporary plans favor grid-based street networks to provide a fine-grained, pedestrian-friendly network with small neighborhood parks at half-mile intervals.

Orenco Station in Hillsboro, Oregon, is a recognized model of this type of TOD pattern (see the case study in Chapter 2). Originally planned for low-density residential development, Orenco Station was then designated as a TOD in the region's transportation and growth management plans. Under its new designation, Orenco Station was to be a compact, pedestrian-oriented, mixed-use neighborhood of high-density housing, employment, and retail located close to transit.[26] In this development, many of the patterns of TODs came together. The commercial services, located in a four-block area around a main street and a regional roadway, provide numerous essential services and a few restaurants in approximately 100,000 square feet.[27] The development achieves an average housing density of 12 dwellings per acre, triple that of the surrounding developments. Several forms of higher-density housing surround the center, including lofts over retail, live-work stacked townhouses, standard townhouses, and apartments. Beyond that, small-lot, single-family and duplex housing completes the development.

The nearby Intel and Toshiba plants, located north and southeast (respectively) of Orenco Station, provide jobs, as do several other, smaller business and research parks. About 18 percent of Orenco Station residents always commute to work by transit; however, this is not an exceptionally high number by Portland standards. Perhaps more significantly, 69 percent of the residents report an increase in the use of transit since moving to Orenco Station.[28] Overall, Orenco Station demonstrates a model for creating higher-density, walkable neighborhoods in suburban locations. Specifically, it is a popular and very marketable TOD that has modestly succeeded at reducing its suburban dwellers' reliance on vehicle travel. It is a step in the right direction.

Neighborhood Diversity

Diversity is a measure of ecological health that also applies to neighborhoods. Ecologists have established that a healthier ecosystem will have more plant and animal diversity. In a similar vein, diversity in neighborhoods would imply a physical diversity capable of supporting a diverse human population. Lively, fine-grained, diverse, and self-perpetuating urban areas are generally the models to which urban designers aspire. In a neighborhood, much of the environmental diversity will be generated from the neighborhood center, where a multitude of shops, services, and businesses are near a diverse array of housing types. The mixed-use center has become the common planning tool aimed at achieving this vibrant diversity, a major challenge of urban design (Figure 5.9).[29]

Both the new urbanism and smart growth movements recommend a mixed-use center that allows flexible zoning and a diversity of uses.[30] Mixing land uses is smart growth's primary principle, while creating a diversity of housing choices (types and costs) is third on the list.[31] Mixing uses in neighborhood centers allows an array of retail, entertainment, business, medical, and social services to coexist there. The greater the diversity of uses that are located in a small area, the more people can do on foot. *New Urban News* has designated mixed-use retail areas as "main street retail," after the shopping streets in many small towns and streetcar suburbs. These shopping districts are characterized by small retail establishments situated along a pedestrian-oriented street. Larger anchor stores, which are generally needed to attract sufficient customers, may be located on a street corner or street end or behind street-front shops. Many cities are now requiring the presence of retail space along designated shopping streets, and some also require or encourage office and residential space above the ground-floor retail.

Orenco Station's shopping streets follow this model. Located along the north side of a major arterial roadway, the shopping and mixed-use district is approximately one block deep and four blocks long. A shopping street on the primary north-south axis of the neighborhood forms the center of the district (Figures 5.9 and 5.10). Buildings within the district are two or three stories, with retail at grade and offices and dwellings above. Within this area are most of the weekly services the residents need, including a grocery store, restaurants and coffee shops, specialty shops, dry cleaners, an optician, a dentist, a psychologist, a stockbroker, and title and real estate offices.[32] (As of 2002, residents listed the following services as still needed: bars/pubs, hair salons, a movie theatre, a post office, bookstores, a gas station, a health center, a veterinarian, and a video store.)[33] Surface parking for shoppers is located on the streets and behind the buildings along alleys. Immediately surrounding the neighborhood service center is a layer of walk-up townhouses and apartments extending approximately a quarter mile from the center (Figure 5.11).

Blocks adjacent to the shopping street often provide the greatest opportunities for complexity and diversity. This is where

Figure 5.9 Orenco Station: the mixed-use neighborhood center.

Figure 5.10 Orenco Station: a shopping street in the neighborhood center.

Figure 5.11 Orenco Station: townhomes with work spaces at the ground level and dwellings above.

higher-density housing can mix with an array of support services, such as medical and professional offices, hardware stores, galleries, and restaurants. In these blocks, transitions from mixed-use to more explicit housing can occur. For example, the village center for Fairview Salem, a neighborhood planned for Salem, Oregon, exemplifies a mixed-use center in which principles of fine grain, flexibility, and diversity drove the planning. The ecologically based plan primarily strives for economic and social diversity, a goal designers hope to achieve by encouraging a variety of building types and scales to accommodate many uses, including an assortment of shops, services, medical and professional offices, a post office, social clubs, and churches. The planners will encourage economic diversity in the population by accommodating a wide range of housing types and costs, from rental apartments to single-family homes. Business—and thus job—diversity is also a goal. The plan encourages both office and light industry development, some of which will occupy existing buildings. In the village center and in the nearby redevelopment area, planners intend to attract many small ecofriendly businesses, such as organic food processors, specialty products, and small-scale fabricators (Figure 5.12).

Compact development patterns in complete, diverse communities reduce the ecological footprint per household. Compactness also affords greater conservation of land and landscape character, reduced loss and fragmentation of natural resource areas, and fewer impervious surfaces. Compactness complemented by completeness increases the opportunities to choose transportation other than automobiles, thus reducing air pollution. Specifically, compact development encourages higher rates of walking and cycling, which leads to improved health. Diversity of land uses and housing types provides a context for more vibrant, diverse, and livable neighborhoods.

Compact gray fabric can perform even better environmentally when it is considered an integral part of the city's green fabric. The gray can in fact be green when buildings and sites are designed to conserve or even create energy; to conserve, reuse,

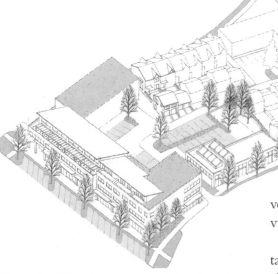

Figure 5.12 Fairview: conceptual drawing of a mixed-use block in the village center.

and cleanse water; and to actively engage vegetation that will perform environmental services.

Gray Fabric Strategies

- Design compact and complete neighborhoods. Residential densities should be 12 to 30 persons per acre in low-rise areas and 75 to 100 persons per acre in mid- to high-rise areas.
- Make neighborhood services too close to drive to. Establish a fine-grain, diverse, pedestrian-oriented neighborhood service center in the heart of every neighborhood, within walking distance of most dwellings. Cluster compatible schools, churches, and recreational uses nearby.
- Encourage neighborhood complexity and diversity. Surround the commercial and service center with a flexibly zoned area able to accommodate a fine-grained mix of residential and smaller-scale commercial uses.
- Include a diverse mix of housing types and densities serving a broad cross section of households.
- Maximize ground-oriented family housing in most neighborhoods.

Chapter 6
Green Fabric

Trees are the oldest and largest living things on the earth, and they are a good measure of the health and quality of our environment. Trees are the original multi-taskers. [They] provide social, ecological, and economic benefits. Their beauty inspires writers and artists, while their leaves and roots clean the air we breathe and the water we drink.

American Forests Web site, http://www.americanforests.org (2005)

The term "green fabric" refers to a city's vegetated lands. It is everywhere that plants grow. Unlike the gray fabric, the green fabric exists throughout the city—crossing the borders of green and gray, networks and fabric (Figure 6.1). Much of it, especially trees, grows along streets and even on buildings, traversing a continuum from natural to highly managed. Along the green networks, it often exists in its most natural state, whereas on rooftops, balconies, and along downtown streets, it is in its most cultured state. Green fabric also crosses public-private boundaries, from public streets and parks to private gardens. As a whole, it creates a unique ecosystem, one in which people have a heavy hand. Green fabric is synonymous with the broadest definitions of urban forest.

While the term "urban forest" is often used to refer only to the city's trees, it is much more, encompassing all of the trees and related woody vegetation in a city.[1] Just as rural forests are understood to be ecosystems—some highly managed, some much less so—urban forests are also ecosystems, composed not only of all urban vegetation but also of soils and related microorganisms, insects, wildlife, and humans.[2] Urban forest ecosystems are unique in the degree to which they reside in a built environment and are controlled by people; as such, they are perhaps closer to a garden than to a forest. The urban forest is a vast area of cultured trees, shrubs, and herbaceous plants, interspersed with tiny remnants of natural landscapes. Even as a heavily managed resource, it provides important environmental services to the city.

While cities grow in population and extent, their environmental

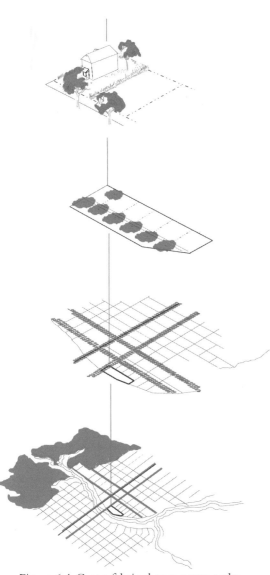

Figure 6.1 Green fabric shown across scales.

impacts amplify even more. The total ecological footprint, or impact, of the average Canadian was estimated in 1991 to be 10.6 acres, the average American's was 12.6 acres, and the average footprint of a person in India was 1 acre. For an American city of 2 million people, the footprint would be 25.2 million acres, an area the size of Kentucky.[3] Yet, as cities grow, their forest canopy typically declines. American Forests has documented losses of forest canopies over twenty- to thirty-year spans. In 1998, the tree canopy cover of Dade County, Florida, for example, was estimated to be only 10 percent. That of Milwaukee, Wisconsin, was estimated at 16 percent. Between 1972 and 1996 in the Puget Sound region, areas with greater than 50 percent canopy cover decreased by 37 percent, from 1.64 million acres to 1.04 million acres. The lost value in air pollution mitigation for the Puget Sound region was estimated to be $95 million.[4] Between 1972 and 2000, in the Willamette/Lower Columbia regions of Oregon and Washington, average tree cover in the region's urban areas dropped from 21 percent to 12 percent, and the lost value for stormwater mitigation for that region was estimated to be $2.4 billion.[5]

Urban forests, the environmental workhorses of cities, have the potential to vastly diminish the negative environmental impacts of urbanization while serving many other important functions. Urban populations are probably most cognizant of the greening and shading roles of trees. Through day-to-day experience, most residents recognize the invaluable capacity of trees to ameliorate extreme climate conditions. Trees provide shade in hot weather and a temporary respite from rain. Hedges and hedgerows block the wind. Most urban populations also place a high value on the aesthetic contributions of urban vegetation (Figure 6.2). The dominant green color is the presence of—and, perhaps more important, symbolizes—nature in the city.[6] For most people, vegetation softens the brutality of the built environment, emphasizing the changing seasons and representing our undeniable relationship to nature. Researchers, including Stephen and Rachael Kaplan and Roger Ulrich, have clearly established the important psychological benefits of vegetation and views of "nature" for urban populations.[7] Donald Appleyard writes: "Apart from the sky, and sometimes water, trees are the primary and last representatives of nature in the city. In this sense, they are a constant

Figure 6.2 Trees in Quincy Market in Boston, Massachusetts.

reminder, not only of the world out there beyond the city, but of our distant past."[8]

The urban forest plays a well-known role in mitigating air pollution. Trees absorb gaseous pollutants, intercept particulates, reduce ozone, and sequester carbon dioxide.[9] The process of photosynthesis enables trees, through their leaves and needles, to filter and sequester carbon and polluting gases as well as significant amounts of particulates from the air. Some research estimates that a street lined with healthy trees can reduce airborne dust particles by as much as 7,000 particles per liter of air.[10] The larger the tree, the more carbon it can store. The large, mature tree canopy in older areas of Sacramento, for example, stores 2,343 kilograms of carbon per tree (approximately 69 tons per acre), whereas smaller trees in the suburban areas store only 24 percent of that per tree (17 tons per acre).[11]

Healthy urban forests can reduce urban energy costs and moderate the urban heat island by shading, or blocking, the sun's radiation. Heavy canopy trees can block up to 95 percent of incoming radiation. Shading buildings and parking lots helps to reduce the need for air-conditioning, while shading outdoor areas helps to keep air temperatures lower in urban areas (Figure 6.3). Three well-placed shade trees around a house can cut air-conditioning energy needs by 10 to 50 percent. Conversely, well-placed trees can also reduce wind speeds and thus moderate heating needs in cold climates.[12] Trees also reduce urban temperatures through evapotranspiration. The process by which plants release water vapor, evapotranspiration utilizes heat energy, increases humidity, and results in a net heat loss throughout the day.[13] This process consumes solar energy that might otherwise heat the air. A single tree can transpire up to 100 gallons of water a day during the growing season. Because each gallon transpired consumes heat energy, this has the same effect as running five average air conditioners for twenty hours.[14]

Urban forests also provide ecological benefits, such as providing wildlife habitat, conserving soil, and enhancing biodiversity.[15] Trees provide habitat for urban wildlife, including insects, birds, and small mammals. They supply food,

Figure 6.3 Temperature drops and humidity increases under a forest canopy.

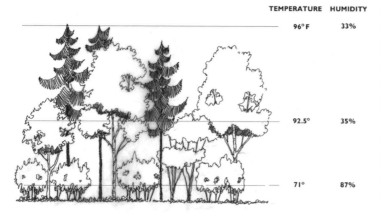

	TEMPERATURE	HUMIDITY
	96°F	33%
	92.5°	35%
	71°	87%

nesting sites, and safe havens for these creatures. Although virtually all of the urban forest supports urban wildlife, remnant forests
and wetlands, left over from predevelopment landscapes, likely
provide the most intact, valuable habitat for native species in urbanized areas. The more linked these patches of habitat are, the
healthier an urban ecosystem is assumed to be and the more
likely it is to support a diversity of plant and animal species.[16] Yet,
even in the most developed contexts, a continuous canopy of
trees can provide airborne travel corridors for some creatures,
keeping them out of harm's way.

Urban Forest as Green Infrastructure

Urban foresters were among the first natural resource professionals to use the term "green infrastructure" to refer to the important environmental work that the urban forest performs for the
city.[17] Whereas urban forestry prior to the 1990s focused on managing the city's public trees, contemporary urban forestry is taking a more ecologically based approach, in which the forest is
managed for both human and ecological functions. Using green
infrastructure as a concept aligns the forest with other urban infrastructure, such as water and sewer systems. The concept recognizes that urban forests can and should perform environmental services—that they should contribute to the urban ecosystem.
The green infrastructure concept holds that the urban forest
should be managed as a healthy ecosystem, using concepts of
process and change, biodiversity, interconnectedness, and economy of means as the basis for environmental health.[18] Understood as green infrastructure, the urban forest is a interwoven system of landscapes performing multiple human and natural
functions.

Trees are the canopy layer, or umbrella, of the urban ecosystem. They exist as part of the city's natural ecosystems but also
extend into the most artificial areas of the city. Trees are the layer
of the urban forest that clearly steps out of natural contexts, such
as greenways and parks, and across the developed areas. In downtown or industrial areas, shopping centers, and strip malls, to
name a few, trees are the only enduring landscape elements—
stepping stones across and through built-up areas. Trees and their

landscaped understory (where it exists) must perform environmental services in the most developed areas of cities. They play multiple roles in this context, one of the most important being to mitigate stormwater runoff.

Research is now emerging that quantifies the role trees play in detaining and filtering stormwater runoff, encouraging infiltration, and dissipating rainfall. Tree canopies intercept rainfall, allowing some to re-evaporate while drips are absorbed into the root system (Figure 6.4).[19] The higher the percentage of forest, trees, and other permeable surfaces, the less runoff that reaches piped drainage systems, reducing erosion and flooding. Thus, treed areas act as detention ponds, slowing the rate at which urban runoff enters streams.[20] In a study in Sacramento, California, a mature, mixed-forest canopy intercepted 36 percent of summer rainfall at the canopy level.[21] A study of a proposed development in Eugene, Oregon, found that when the proposed trees mature, producing a canopy that covers 58 percent of the site, the trees will reduce stormwater peak flows by more than 25 percent in leaf-on conditions.[22]

Root systems and their associated microbes act as sediment filters to trap and break down many stormwater pollutants. Pesticides, fertilizers, petroleum products, and suspended solids all can be either stabilized or taken up by plants. The science of phytoremediation, a biological method of cleaning up toxic lands, has taught us that biological processes occurring in the root zones of plants can remove or neutralize toxins, metals, sediments, minerals, salts, and other pollutants.[23] Plants also stabilize slopes and soils and help prevent construction- and storm-related erosion. For example, in the Gunpowder Falls Basin in the Chesapeake Bay area, forested areas released 50 tons of sediment per square mile per year to the local waters, whereas suburban areas contributed up to twice that amount. Land stripped for construction released 25,000 to 50,000 tons of sediment, or five hundred to one thousand times as much as the forest.[24]

The percentage of land covered by tree canopies can help indicate development impacts. American Forests has developed methods for evaluating general environmental impacts of losing tree canopy area to development. They have also been able to quantify the monetary value to cities of increases or decreases of tree canopy cover relative to cities' requirements to mitigate air

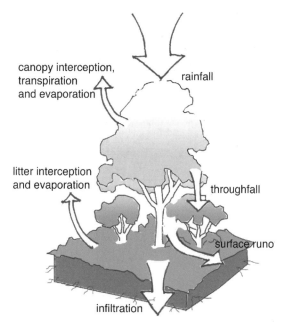

Figure 6.4 Net rainfall entering the soil under a heavy tree canopy. (Source: derived from Bureau of Environmental Services *Clean River Plan*)

and water pollution and stormwater runoff. Based on many analyses of urban ecosystems, American Forests recommends that cities establish targets for tree canopy cover. For cities east of the Mississippi and in the Pacific Northwest they recommend an overall average canopy cover of 40 percent of the land area. For downtown areas, they recommend 15 percent cover; for urban residential areas, 25 percent cover; and for suburban residential areas, 50 percent cover. Lower goals are recommended for cities in the Southwest and the dry West.[25]

Planting Green Streets

The urban forest as broadly defined is the primary tool to be used in restoring a natural urban hydrology. In natural stormwater management practices urban plants and their roots systems are being called on to absorb and filter stormwater runoff in the same way as plants and soils in natural landscapes. Many jurisdictions have implemented new stormwater management codes and standards that require some form of mitigation for impervious surfaces, while some charge stormwater fees based on areas of impervious surfaces. Many stormwater management departments are planning more naturally based approaches to replace or supplement underground piped drainage. Some are running up against street and landscape design standards that essentially prohibit innovative stormwater design. For example, most urban areas require 6-inch curbs along streets for safety reasons. This makes it very difficult to direct water from the street to a roadside swale (gentle ditch) for draining stormwater. Such conflicts are requiring new collaborations to rethink the details of standard urban design.[26]

Metro, the regional planning and policy district for Portland, Oregon, developed a Green Streets program and related guidebook (also see Chapter 4), designed to protect the natural resources being acquired under its regional open spaces program, to adhere to federal and state environmental laws, and to provide education and guidance to the twenty-seven jurisdictions in its metropolitan area. Intended to help public agencies and developers design and build streets that incorporate stormwater treatment and infiltration within the right-of-way, the techniques promoted

Figure 6.5 Green street with stormwater filtration/infiltration in the center median (cross section and plan views). (Source: Metro, *Trees for Green Streets*)

in the guidebook include reducing the impervious surfaces associated with streets, planting trees (particularly large-canopy trees) to cover much of the paved areas, and using trees, planting strips, and center medians along streets to control and filter runoff (Figure 6.5). For each stormwater-related problem, a range of solutions is provided. For example, the guidebook explains many drainage swale types and illustrates several choices of curb types that allow water to run into roadside swales. Tree planting along and within streets is emphasized, as are street designs that provide adequate space and growing conditions for large-canopy trees and multiple rows of trees. Stormwater treatment medians include trees interspersed with planted stormwater gardens (planted detention basins). A compendium document, *Trees for Green Streets,* details the functions of and selection and planting details for trees intended for use in green streets or other stormwater mitigation efforts.[27] Green streets that manage their own runoff are clearly an essential component of designing green neighborhoods, and trees are essential components of these streets.

Villebois, in the Portland metropolitan area (see the case study in Chapter 2), uses green streets as part of a broader rainwater management plan, which is designed to not only reduce the impacts of its development but also restore the groundwater system damaged by the former occupant, a state mental hospital. After the citizens of Wilsonville, Oregon, successfully defeated a proposal for a new prison on the property, the state agreed to collaborate with the city and developers on a new mixed-use development for the land. In their successful bid for the project, the developers proposed a smart growth community that would incorporate "cutting edge green development practices and rainwater management techniques."[28] The plan for this 482-acre community includes 154 acres (31 percent of the site) in parks and open spaces. Restoring the pre-development hydrology of the site was a primary objective, in part to assist the goals of ecological restoration and in part to address a water shortage in the city that had previously required a construction moratorium. The Coffee Lake wetlands (71 acres), an extension of Metro-owned land to the north, and two significant forested areas were mandated for protection. Set aside as preserves, they form key habitat patches in an interconnected system of on-site open spaces. The greenway loops through the developed areas following a historic streambed. It also provides stormwater management and recreation and is the primary green corridor, ranging from 150 to 400 feet wide. Set aside first in the planning process, historic wetlands, creeks, and remnant forests largely structured the plan of the community. All three creeks on the site, buried by the former occupants, are to be restored.[29]

Extensive natural landscapes and a rainwater management system are two components of the Villebois greenway system. Several boulevards on the proposed development will include biofiltration swales in center medians (Figure 6.6). A sitewide rainwater management standard requires retention, infiltration, and treatment of 90 percent of the typical winter's rainstorms—drizzle that typically produces a quarter inch of rain or less in twenty-four hours. For these drizzle events, rainfall must be directed to bioretention areas, rainwater gardens, rainwater planters, and vegetated swales. These systems capture the rainfall from all drizzle events and filter 70 percent of suspended solids and 65 percent of phosphorous, a particularly problematic stormwater pollutant in the region. A backup piped system will handle runoff from larger rainfalls, which occur on average once every two to one hundred years.[30]

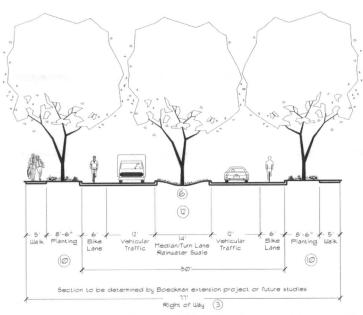

Figure 6.6 Villebois: minor arterial street with a rainwater swale in the center median (cross section view). (Source: Walker Macy et al., *Villebois,* vol. 4)

Trees will be an integral part of these systems. Mitigation for impervious surfaces is required at Villebois, and because trees slow, absorb, and filter runoff, they factor into the stormwater system design. Based on conservative figures (used because trees take time to grow), each deciduous tree, leafless during the rainy season, would mitigate 100 square feet of impervious surface, and each evergreen tree would mitigate 200 square feet. Builders will select their trees from an extensive list provided by the developer and preapproved by the city.[31] A tree-planting plan designates where green streets will be and where the largest trees are required (Figure 6.13). This encoding of trees as viable components of stormwater management systems not only recognizes their true contribution but also will encourage more extensive planting of trees in the future.

Defining Neighborhood Space

> Beyond helping to define a street, separating the pedestrian realm from vehicles, and providing shade, what makes trees so special is their movement; the constant movement of their branches and leaves, and the ever-changing light that plays on, through, and around them.
>
> A. B. Jacobs, *Great Streets*

Urban trees are the principal aesthetic elements of urban outdoor spaces. Many of the world's most famous urban streets and spaces are made memorable by their trees. Around the world, many parks, gardens, campuses, boulevards, streets, and urban spaces receive their defining character from the placement, type, and size of their trees (Figure 6.7). In Paris, the Champs Élysées, the most famous street in the world according to author Allan Jacobs, is a boulevard that is defined by its trees (particularly between Rond-Point and the Place de la Concorde).[32] London plane trees line the street edge; further back, double rows of elms form a bosk that marks the outside edge of a spacious public realm. In Beijing, China, multiple rows of trees, each row a different species and often a different age, line the edges of streets to create both a grand scale and layered edges. Many of Beijing's streets exhibit very close spacing of trees, creating a fully canopied

Figure 6.7 Tree-lined streets radiating from the Arc de Triomphe in Paris.

character.[33] Some American streets distinctive for their trees include Benjamin Franklin Parkway in Philadelphia, Royal Palm Way in Palm Beach, Florida, and innumerable residential streets, such as those in old Savannah, Georgia. Certain urban spaces, including Bryant Park and Paley Park in New York, are also made captivating by their trees.[34]

In all of these memorable urban spaces, trees complement built structures in creating and defining outdoor rooms and corridors. Trees subtly establish spatial boundaries (e.g., edges and canopies), create rhythms to heighten outdoor experience, and give urban spaces a sense of scale. They express the seasons with their leaves and flowers and record time by their growth.[35] The orderly qualities of deciduous trees or what we have come to know as "street" trees—tall, columnar trunks topped by spreading canopies—makes them exemplary complements to built structure in the urban environment. They mitigate a transition between the order of building interiors and the ill-defined out-of-doors. By emphasizing and extending the geometry of buildings and of the street system in the city, trees create a comfortable vestibule between interior and outdoor environments. They define and subdivide space by enclosing rooms within larger spaces or simply creating subspaces under their canopies, and they connect spaces by creating corridors along parks, plazas, or street edges (Figure 6.8).[36]

Beyond the urban core of most North American cities, the size and density of buildings diminish, and these buildings do little to define street and pedestrian spaces. Particularly in low-density areas, where buildings are eclectic in design, widely spaced, and set back from the street, trees and other landscape elements (e.g., hedges) become the primary tools for defining and subdividing public space.[37] In fact, in the residential environment, a street lined with majestic, full-canopied trees is a quintessential image of a "good" neighborhood. Examples exist in virtually any North American city; a few notable examples include the streets of Riverside near Chicago, Monument Avenue in Richmond, Virginia, and Orange Grove Boulevard in Pasadena, California.[38] Of Riverside, designer Frederick Law Olmsted wrote: "A tasteful and convenient disposition of shade trees, and other plantings along the road-sides and public places, will, in a few years, cause the whole locality . . . to possess, not only the attraction of neatness and convenience, and the charm of refined sylvan beauty and

Figure 6.8 Trees define a sitting area at Battery Park City, New York, New York.

Figure 6.9 A pedestrian corridor created by closely spaced red maples on Robson Street in Vancouver, British Columbia, designed by Cornelia Hahn Oberlander.

grateful umbrageousness, but an aspect of secluded peacefulness and tranquility."[39]

In the residential environment, trees and the adjacent sidewalk are what declare the street to be public space and what subdivide it into a series of corridor-like rooms—with the smaller, edge spaces under the tree canopy and along the sidewalk for pedestrians and the larger space along the road for vehicles. Even young trees planted in lines, with relatively close and consistent spacing, begin to define the street space. With maturity, they will make the street a gracious outdoor room. To subdivide the street right-of-way into zones or rooms effectively or (to use a building metaphor) to line the street with a colonnade (of trees), street trees must be spaced closely. Similarly, to provide a canopy of branches and leaves to walk under, the trees have to be planted closely (Figure 6.9). According to urban designers, such as Allan Jacobs and Henry Arnold, trees lose their visual effectiveness and can fail at the job of spatial definition when they are planted more than 30 feet apart.[40] This, in turn, demands that the street design include adequate space and growing conditions to nurture healthy trees and that urban forest design be an early, proactive component of neighborhood design.

New or redeveloped neighborhoods are our modern-day opportunity to create great twenty-first-century streets. In new communities, the street system, the open space system, and parks are designed in advance. The opportunity exists to design the street with trees playing a major space-defining role from the outset. The heavy emphasis in smart growth and new urbanist communities on creating positive, comfortable pedestrian streets establishes a major role for trees. They appear prominently in many illustrations of these communities and are a requirement in the design standards of most. In a few new communities, trees play an even larger role related to neighborhood identity and way finding. Garrison Woods and Villebois are two redevelopment projects that deserve specific mention for their extraordinary efforts to preserve existing trees and to feature trees as significant components of urban design.

Garrison Woods is an inner-city redevelopment of a Canadian Forces base in Calgary, Alberta. The developers, Canada Lands, worked closely with the City of Calgary and surrounding neighborhoods to design a new neighborhood that would knit into the surrounding areas, preserve and restore housing stock from the base, and also preserve some of the existing landscape, particularly the trees. At the same time, it would create a new neighborhood of much higher density, with schools, parks, and neighborhood commercial services. Garrison Woods was sited on a primarily residential portion of the former base, a neighborhood composed of two-story duplex officers' housing. The need to increase density while creating single-family home sites made it impossible to keep all streets in their prior location. However, efforts were made to align some new streets with previous ones to retain mature trees. Some of the most notable trees on the private lots were protected as well (Figure 6.10). Grand Boulevard, the main street through the neighborhood, was the most significant effort and success in tree protection. City of Calgary staff in parks planning and urban forestry worked hard on behalf of the developers to convince the city's engineering staff to modify street design standards. The result was a skinny street with parking that is occasionally interrupted by sidewalks that meander to avoid large trees. Put together with renovated older homes and traditionally styled new homes, the street provided an immediate feeling of an established neighborhood the summer it was completed.

Designers of Villebois, in Wilsonville, Oregon, had an even grander scheme for the development's urban forest. In addition to the significant efforts at habitat preservation (discussed earlier in this chapter), designers conceived the urban forest early in the design process as contributing strongly to the identity of "the village near the woods," as promotional literature dubs it.[41] Intended to address the three core principles of the Villebois concept—connectivity, diversity, and sustainability—a tree plan was created in the earliest phases of design. Both existing and newly planted trees play a significant urban design role in the project.[42]

The Dammasch hospital, the original site of Villebois, was constructed in 1958. Most of the hospital site was landscaped in turf, ornamental trees, and shrubs. These forty-five-year-old trees were recognized as a valuable resource by the city, who encouraged the developers of the project to preserve as much of the existing urban forest on the site as possible.[43] Costa Pacific and their designers embraced the idea of maximizing tree preservation. A detailed tree survey was completed, locating all existing trees on

Figure 6.10 Garrison Woods: a renovated street with many preserved trees.

Figure 6.11 Villebois: trees that will be preserved in the redevelopment of the site.

Figure 6.12 Villebois: the Village Center plaza, sited around magnificent mature trees. (Source: Fletcher Farr Ayotte)

the site and describing and evaluating them for size, species, health, and structure as well as factoring in their historical importance. Throughout the design and construction process, efforts were made to preserve most of the "important" or "good" trees (Figure 6.11). For example, in refining the neighborhood plan, parks and other open spaces were sited around significant trees. Two streets in the new development were aligned with old ones to preserve the street trees, and the Village Center was sited to take advantage of some particularly majestic trees (Figures 6.12 and 6.13). The greenway was enlarged to include several clusters of mature trees, including some native Oregon white oaks. Hilltop Park was located on a historic homestead site, which contained a massive bigleaf maple, English walnuts, and the original hedgerow of Douglas fir and cedar. On private lands, trees will be protected under the city's stringent tree protection standards, which require a tree protection plan for each component of the development and oversight throughout the construction process by a certified arborist.[44]

The plan addressed Metro's green streets guidelines by including bioswales along several major streets and by emphasizing the use of large canopy trees. To provide continuity, such preferred trees as oak, elm, beech, and plane trees were selected for each of the major streets leading into and around the community. For example, the Loop Road, which aligns the greenway and two parks, will be lined with tulip trees, whereas the arterials that cross through the middle of the site will be lined with Accolade elm. Designers addressed diversity by establishing a list of more than twenty-two tree species (with several varieties of each to avoid monocultures) and by encouraging the use of native plants and those that would provide habitat.[45] The efforts made to preserve natural areas and trees, and to establish a substantial tree canopy cover over time, addressed sustainability in terms of the significant role the trees would eventually play in both stormwater and air quality mitigation. Taken together, the attention to landscape preservation, stormwater management geared toward repairing site hydrology, and an intentionally designed urban forest, Villebois provides a clear example of landscape as green infrastructure.

Set within the context of Portland's Metropolitan Greenspaces plan and the related green streets guidelines, Villebois demonstrates how the urban forest can play significant green infrastructure and urban design roles concurrently in new community design. The multifunctional role for the urban forest was conceived at the earliest stages of visualizing the development and, in fact, shaped the plan. No less important was the context of a long-range regional program of green networks and strong local tree preservation laws. The intentional and early design of the urban forest for multiple functions is a key component of green neighborhood design.

Figure 6.13 Villebois: street tree plan. (Source: Walker Macy et al., *Villebois,* vol. 4)

Green Fabric Strategies

- Plant, grow, and nurture a healthy, sustainable urban forest, one that contributes to civic beauty and to a healthy urban ecosystem.
- Plan the urban forest as a keystone component of green networks.
- Preserve remnant forests and mature trees.
- Set a goal of 40 percent tree canopy cover.
- Use the urban forest to help conserve, clean, and manage urban water.
- Use trees to structure memorable, distinctive urban spaces.
- Give high priority to street trees; design the new urban forest early and for longevity.

Chapter 7
Urban Water

Understanding water—truly understanding how it works, where it goes, what it feels like, what it means, how it is used, how it sounds, tastes and smells—is an essential first step toward gaining a real awareness of site and region.

K. W. Rinne, "Hydroscape/Cityscape"

Simply put, urban water is all the water that lives under, falls upon, and flows through a city. It includes rainfall, groundwater, river or stream water, water used by industry, water for irrigation, and drinking water that is pumped up or piped in and purified for human consumption. Urban water also includes the outputs—sewage, industrial wastewater, and stormwater. The urban water most obviously affected by urban development is stormwater runoff. Composed mostly of rainfall, stormwater also includes runoff from irrigation, and sometimes illegal inputs to the stormwater system (such as drainage from sump pumps). The focus of this chapter is urban stormwater runoff (the city's surface waters), including its problems and the potential to rehabilitate a damaged urban hydrology (Figure 7.1).

North American cities typically use water from nearby natural sources, such as lakes, rivers, or underlying groundwater. It is purified before it is used by the city's inhabitants, providing the "potable" water supply; once used, it is typically considered "wastewater." In the United States, the Clean Water Act requires this wastewater to be recleaned before it is returned to lakes, streams, and rivers. However, it is rarely purified to match the temperature, chemistry, and clarity of clean natural water. Perhaps more significant these days, one of the dirtiest components of urban water, stormwater runoff, has until recently been ignored as a source of pollution. As a result, most rivers, streams, and lakes that are the recipients of urban wastewater are highly polluted. It is estimated that 70 percent of urban water pollution in the United States is due to stormwater runoff.[1]

Development typically involves building and paving over vast

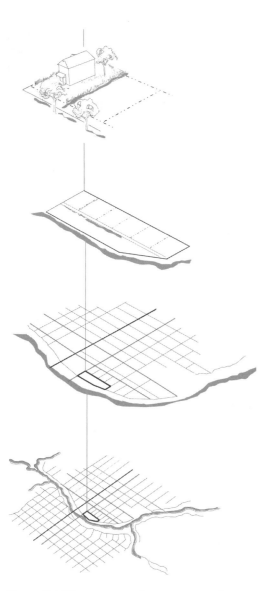

Figure 7.1 Water systems shown across scales.

areas of land. Typical urban development covers from 40 percent to 95 percent of the land with roofs and paving, known as impervious surfaces. This extensive conversion of the landscape from mostly roughly textured, pervious cover to smooth, impervious surfaces dramatically affects the local hydrology. For example, a typical new suburban house on a 6,000-square-foot lot replaces almost half of the site with impervious roofs and paving. A typical shopping mall replaces more than 95 percent of its site with roofs and paving. Urbanized landscapes generate higher volumes of runoff at faster rates than their agricultural or natural counterparts because so little of the rainfall can filter into the ground.

Exacerbating this situation is the piped urban stormwater system common to North American cities. As rain falls on the city, it hits these impervious surfaces and runs to nearby collection points. From these points, an underground network of pipes directs the water to nearby lakes, streams, and rivers. The objective of these stormwater management systems has been to collect and direct urban stormwater runoff out of town as quickly as possible—to keep the city dry and comfortable for its inhabitants. The resulting volume and velocity of water entering natural water systems coupled with pollutants—such as pesticides, herbicides, fertilizers, petroleum products, and suspended solids—picked up along the way has serious negative impacts on natural water systems. This urban stormwater erodes waterways, increases algae growth, increases stream temperatures and sedimentation, and decreases available oxygen for fish and other aquatic life.[2]

Rushing the stormwater out of cities also depletes the groundwater within urban areas. Although rainfall volumes vary dramatically from landscape to landscape and from season to season, groundwater is a ubiquitous, crucial component of the hydrologic cycle. A far more stable resource than surface water, groundwater typically remains a consistent temperature and its levels (relative to the ground plane) vary slowly from rainstorm to rainstorm and season to season. It is a crucial source of water for trees and other large woody vegetation, and it provides a stable source of water for lakes, streams, and rivers.[3] By capturing stormwater from impervious surfaces and piping it to streams, rivers, and lakes, cities that utilize these conventional stormwater management systems deplete their groundwater resources.

In the United States, the Environmental Protection Agency

(EPA) is mandated under the 1972 Clean Water Act to maintain the nation's waters in a clean and healthy state. Between 1972 and 1987, the focus of the nation's cleanup efforts was "point source" pollution, primarily industrial and urban wastewater treatment. However, by the mid-1980s, another very significant source of water pollution was recognized—what the agency calls "non-point source" pollution, primarily agricultural and urban runoff. Such diffuse sources of pollution accumulate from distributed sources, including automobile-related oil and sediment, lawn care–related pesticides and herbicides, erosion from construction sites, yard and pet waste, deposition of atmospheric pollutants, trash, and other pollutants resulting from daily urban activities.

The detailed list and the behaviors of biological, chemical, and temperature pollutants associated with urban runoff are complex. The tolerance levels of wildlife species to these pollutants are the subject of much study as federal and state agencies attempt to establish maximum allowable pollutant levels to comply with clean water and endangered species regulations. What has been established thus far is that these pollutants contribute to significant losses of aquatic species in runoff-polluted waterways. For example, a recent study of several partially restored streams in the Seattle, Washington, area concluded that spawning salmon were not surviving in the streams long enough to reproduce. Although not proven, the culprit was suspected to be high levels of polluted urban runoff that entered the streams on a regular basis.[4]

Since the amendment of the Clean Water Act in 1987 to address nonpoint source pollution, the EPA has been directed to regulate and help local jurisdictions to manage the water pollution associated with runoff. Through the National Pollutant Discharge Elimination System, the EPA is encouraging pollution prevention and requiring that minimum standards be met for stormwater discharges. Currently, communities of more than 50,000 people must implement a minimum of six "Best Management Practices" (or BMPs). These include public education and outreach on stormwater impacts, public participation, detection and elimination of illicit discharge, control of construction site runoff, postconstruction stormwater management, and pollution prevention for municipal operations.[5] In implementing the Clean Water Act, some states have gone further by establishing more specific standards, such as maximum allowable pollutant levels for lakes, streams, and rivers. While this federal and state regulation will go a long way toward fixing the problems of urban water, the focus of the Clean Water Act is eliminating water pollution; thus, it does not address the entire problem of water hydrology. It overlooks problems associated with water volumes and excessive peak flows during rainstorms and also pays little attention to the problems of depleted groundwater that are associated with piping runoff out of cities.

In some areas of the United States, the Endangered Species Act of 1973 is also influencing the management of urban hydrology. As one example, in 1999 the National Marine Fisheries Service listed certain species of salmon as threatened or endangered in nine watersheds of the Pacific Northwest, including several in urban areas.[6] An endangered species listing means that listed species and their habitat are protected by law and that actions that negatively affect the species or their habitat are punishable by jail terms and fines. Many urban development practices, such as removing riparian vegetation, building road crossings, and (worse yet) filling streams, would clearly degrade urban fish habitat. Seattle, Portland, and many smaller Pacific Northwest cities affected by this listing began to implement measures to protect fish-bearing streams and rivers. In metropolitan Portland, the regional planning authority (Metro) adopted Title 3 to protect water quality and floodplain resources as part of its growth management plan.[7] Metro recommends generous buffers along what they call protected water features as well as erosion control measures and stormwater filtration throughout the metropolitan area. Passing the ordinance also led to Metro's Green Streets program (see Chapter 4) to reduce road impacts on waterways. Together, the Clean Water Act and the endangered species listings are leading many northwestern cities to explore a nature-based approach to managing urban hydrology. Since 1999, much planning effort in these cities has been directed toward establishing development practices and stormwater management methods to reduce urban impacts on stream and river habitat.

Sustaining Urban Water

We must change the role of stormwater. It can now be seen as a resource replenishing the urban stream networks that host myriad human activities and abundant plant and wildlife communities. We can cease to perceive stormwater as a waste, burdening the quality and quantity of water draining into our lakes and streams. Stormwater does not have to be the source of disease and floods that it was in the nineteenth century.

W. E. Wenk and C. Gregg, "Stormwater Gardens"

The earth's natural water cycle sustains life on this planet. On the global scale, rain condenses from clouds, falls to the ground, makes its way across the land and underground to rivers, lakes, and oceans, and evaporates into the atmosphere; then the cycle begins again. At the scale of a small watershed, rain falling on a forested environment is intercepted by vegetation. Some beads up on leaves or needles and evaporates before it reaches the ground. The balance drips to the ground or runs down the trunk and is captured in layers of duff, which store much of it for extended periods of time. Rain that eventually reaches the soil layers slowly infiltrates and makes it way to air pockets throughout the active soil layers. Some of this former rain becomes groundwater that slowly moves underground toward nearby streams. Some runs overland, meandering over rough terrain as sheet flow until it finds a low area, where it gathers to become a tiny first-order stream. These tiny streams flow together to become higher-order streams until the water eventually reaches a river, lake, wetland, or estuary.

The time it takes a drop to travel from the canopy of a tree to a second- or third-order stream is considerable, and significant amounts of rainfall evaporate or are taken up by plants and soil before reaching the first stream. On average, 30 percent of the rainfall on a forest is absorbed into the spongelike ground and slowly moves underground toward surface water systems. Only about 3.5 percent flows overland as surface runoff. Below the ground, vast quantities of groundwater are stored. This groundwater maintains moisture in soils as well as small volumes of water year-round in most streams. According to University of Georgia professor Bruce Ferguson, the volume of water stored in soil layers in most natural watersheds exceeds the quantities that could be stored in dammed reservoirs or the typical detention basins that many cities require.[8]

As with many of the systems that sustain urban life, urban hydrology can be healthier. A more natural, healthier urban hydrology would mimic local healthy watersheds. How the rainfall behaves and how the vegetation has adapted to local soils and hydrologic environments provide models. However, natural watersheds cannot simply be copied in the urban environment, which is very different. The fundamental differences—vast areas of pavement and roofs, little open land, high pollutant levels, and higher temperatures—together create a different environment and require adaptive approaches to an urban hydrologic cycle (Figure 7.2).

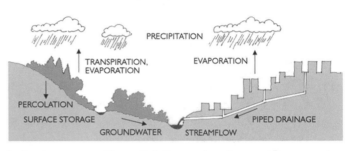

Figure 7.2 Comparison between the natural (left) and the urban (right) hydrologic cycles.

Well before the EPA officially recognized the problem of urban stormwater, landscape architects Anne Spirn and Michael Hough separately addressed the problems with conventional urban stormwater management and described more naturally based approaches to managing urban waters. The fundamental principle proposed by both authors was to understand and manage all urban waters as components of the water cycle. Thus, water falling on or used by the city should, first and foremost, be captured and used, then cleaned and reused in a cyclical manner. In terms of rainfall, the first principle was to capture, treat, and maximize either the use of this water or its infiltration to the ground, rather than shipping it out of the city. The second principle was to make the water cycle visible and tangible to urban residents. Spirn recommended two scales of attention, including planning at the scale of the whole city and water-sensitive design at the site scale. Planning at the city scale would conserve and restore the city's streams and wetlands, and urban development would be planned to allow some natural flooding to occur. About the site scale, she stated: "Every new building, street, parking lot, and park within the city should be designed to prevent or mitigate flooding and to conserve and restore water resources."[9]

Twenty years later, planners and designers of cities are starting to "get it," and stormwater management systems similar to what Spirn and Hough proposed are being constructed. Some engineering professionals have adopted an ecosystem-based approach to stormwater planning, in which the main idea is to protect and augment the natural surface drainage system in a watershed or subwatershed, rather than supplant it with a piped or channeled system.[10] This approach involves first protecting

Figure 7.3 Rain garden at the former offices of Wenk Associates Landscape Architects, Denver, Colorado. (Source: Wenk Associates)

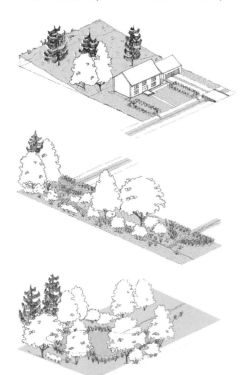

Figure 7.4 A treatment train: stormwater is captured, detained, and filtered in many small gardens, swales, and ponds on the way from the house to the stream.

riparian corridors, wetlands, floodplains, and the forest canopy and forest floor to the extent possible. Then it also replaces lost storage and infiltration capacity of all urban landscapes through the use of stormwater BMPs and such practices as low-impact development and a closely related concept, "infiltration stormwater systems."[11] Both of these approaches strive to maximize the infiltration of rainfall where it falls, rather than allowing it to run overland. Most naturally based stormwater management systems integrate surface drainage and infiltration with numerous other practices, such as green roofs, rain gardens, water storage, and biofiltration, in what some have called a "treatment train" (Figures 7.3 and 7.4).

Pioneering open drainage systems were installed at The Woodlands, Texas (pop. 150,000), and Bellevue, Washington (pop. 100,000), in the 1970s. The system at The Woodlands was initially conceived by Wallace McHarg Roberts and Todd at the conclusion of their environmental analysis conducted in 1974 for a proposed new community. They proposed a system that mimicked the site's natural hydrology by protecting wooded floodplains and area of well-drained soils to store and absorb rainfall. Linked to the site's natural drainage patterns, this system of creeks, wetlands, ponds, and infiltration zones forms a townwide open space system, some of it accessible to the public (Figure 7.5).[12]

Similarly, to combat persistent flooding problems in the rapidly urbanizing suburban city of Bellevue, city officials made a decision in 1973 to protect and enhance its natural system of streams and wetlands, rather than go the way of most communities of the time. To do so, Bellevue acquired land along creeks and around ponds, floodplains, and wetlands. In some of these areas, they installed a system of small check dams that would temporarily store floodwater during storms. Bellevue's drainage system is fully integrated with its parks and open space system. Many of the areas are cooperatively managed by the parks and stormwater departments to serve stormwater, recreation, and environmental purposes concurrently.[13]

Natural drainage systems such as Bellevue's provide multiple ecological and social benefits. Because protection of existing riparian corridors is an important component of natural drainage, these systems help protect natural vegetation and habitat. For example, Kelsey and Coal creeks in Bellevue continue to support salmon populations. These systems also provide natural scenic values, passive recreation, environmental education, and alternate transportation (Figure 7.6). The intentional integration of a natural stormwater management system with parks and open spaces yields significant synergistic benefits. In a comparison of Bellevue with two adjacent suburban cities, Redmond and Renton, Bellevue had ten times more miles of off-road trails than its two neighbors, largely because of these protected, multipurpose green networks. The open drainage systems at The Woodlands and at Bellevue cost less than conventional piped and channeled systems to install, perform exceptionally well under potential flooding conditions, and concurrently provide multiple other benefits. Both have survived storms in excess of one-hundred-year levels (The Woodlands in 1979 and 1994; Bellevue in 1984 and 1990) with very little damage to private or public property.

Just as the hydrologic balance of any ecosystem is crucial to its healthy functioning, so too can urban hydrology contribute to a more environmentally sustainable community. Ecological restoration was a driving principle for the new development of Coffee Creek Center near the city of Chesterton, Indiana, and water management played a central role in this effort (see the case study in Chapter 2). A natural drainage system was designed to help restore portions of the site to presettlement conditions. This new sustainable community in the Duneland area of northwestern Indiana is described by lead planner and architect William McDonough as a "green world with connecting gray zones.[14]" Of the 675-acre site, 225 acres will be preserved as open space and parks. The heart of the "green world" is the Coffee Creek Watershed Preserve, a 600-foot-wide, 175-acre landscape preservation zone that bisects the development. The preserve is being resurrected from a very disturbed stream corridor and its adjacent wetlands and woodlands. Using historic ecological information, the Coffee Creek Watershed Conservancy will lead the effort to reestablish native plant communities through long-term management.[15]

The "water management system" was designed by German water systems consultants Atelier Dreiseitl, who are noted for artistic urban waterworks that utilize stormwater runoff. This system is designed to help restore the hydrologic balance and ecosystem of Coffee Creek and its buffer. Described as the project's "lifeblood," the stormwater system will mitigate the future

Figure 7.5 A water infiltration area near a hotel at The Woodlands, Texas.

Figure 7.6 A walking trail through a wetland in Lake Hills Greenbelt Park in Bellevue, Washington.

Figure 7.7 Coffee Creek Center: rainwater garden in a residential area.

Figure 7.8 Coffee Creek Center: trails lead to a gazebo overlooking the Coffee Creek Watershed Preserve.

impacts of development by maximizing filtration and infiltration of runoff and controlling quantities of runoff to avoid erosion and sedimentation. Water cleaning and infiltration occur at every scale in the project—on the home site, on the block, and at the development level (Figure 7.7). An underground system of "level spreaders" picks up stormwater that flows out of developed portions of the site and distributes this water to the soil for cleaning and infiltration. All developers are required to address stormwater management by infiltrating water on-site and by connecting to the development-wide management system. Unlike much of Herbert Dreiseitl's European work, the central function of the water system is not equally reflected through intentional art. Rather, it is subtle, naturalistic, and blended with the restoration of the wetland preserve, whose central location and public accessibility will assure its prominent role in defining this sustainable community (Figure 7.8).[16]

Stormwater as Civic Amenity

Since early civilization, water has been the source and subject of art and cultural expression. The ancient Romans, in particular, publicized their ability to provide the populations with clean water through beautiful structures, such as the aqueducts, public fountains, and public baths—all integral parts of classically designed public spaces. This attitude toward celebrating water in grand and ornate displays was revived in the Italian Renaissance. The celebration of water in Renaissance cities was closely linked to function through water provision to the citizenry; to spirituality through iconography or symbolism; and to socialization, as the fountains were the gathering places of each town. Perhaps the clearest examples are the fountains of Renaissance Rome. Connected to a complex gravity-fed water supply system, parts of which date back to ancient times, fountains such as two by Bernini in Piazza Navona were and still are centerpieces of public space. The design of each unique fountain was the product of the artist's interpretation, of the desires of a benefactor, of siting within the urban space, and of geography, which dictated the volume and pressure of available water.[17]

In contemporary cities, water has been widely available and cheap. In response, water features have become common and overused corporate decorations. Many of these features are disconnected from both cultural and religious meaning and from human and environmental function. Many use and waste drinking water. Herbert Dreiseitl observed this in his own commissions: "My first projects were fountains designed for squares in towns and country communities. . . . I was particularly dissatisfied with one very common idea: water as decoration in the townscape, a pleasant toy for artists and architects, but a superfluous one sometimes . . . while all the essential water management in the town, like for example rainwater removal, drinking water provision and sewage disposal is dealt with functionally, scarcely visibly and without any aesthetic sense."[18] His recent work—including such projects as the famous Potsdamer Platz in Berlin and a town square in Kogarah, Australia—focuses on capturing, cleaning, and featuring stormwater as civic art. These works reveal the water cycle in creative displays that change dramatically with and without the presence of water.

American landscape architect William Wenk is known internationally for his artful designs for stormwater management facilities, many of them in public parks. He writes: "Designers must become re-involved in the design of urban infrastructure at the scale of the site and the system. The design of systems requires a pragmatic approach to the development of components that when linked together create systems that address engineering, environmental and civic design issues. . . . For example, we can rethink all components of urban stormwater systems, from individual storm drain inlets to trunk storm sewers, to create surface stormwater systems that are functional and beautiful."[19]

Wenk's Shop Creek restoration project, built in the late 1980s near Aurora, Colorado, exemplifies his approach, which integrates artful design with restorative hydrology. The structure of Shop Creek was severely damaged and phosphorous levels were high because of recent upstream development that had flushed stormwater into the creek. Wenk's design inserted dramatic circular "outcrops" (as Wenk calls them) to reduce water velocities and allow sediments to settle (Figure 7.9).[20] The project also in-

Figure 7.9 A drop structure (designed by Wenk Associates) that dissipates the water's energy is part of the restored Shop Creek in Aurora, Colorado.

cludes restored steam banks, native vegetation that had been replanted, and a public path that aligned the creek.

Urban waterworks can and should perform cultural, aesthetic, environmental, and sometimes recreational functions in concert. In tight urban spaces, they might be works of art that celebrate and clean urban runoff. In the open spaces of the city's green networks, surface and subsurface waters become lynchpin components of the city's green infrastructure, providing water resources for human recreation and education as well as important urban habitat areas. Numerous examples exist of such multipurpose spaces that are equal parts landscape restoration and civic art.

Designed by Hargreaves Associates, Guadalupe River Park in San Jose exemplifies urban riverfront restoration projects that enjoin civic and ecological goals (Figure 7.10). Guadalupe River Park, originally planned to be a conventional Army Corps of Engineers flood control channel, became a striking linear park extending from downtown 3 miles to the airport. With the Hargreaves Associates consulting team, the City of San Jose's Redevelopment Agency challenged the Army Corps' proposal with their more artful and public-oriented scheme. The park, which changes from a sculptural "hardscape" downtown to a naturalistic restored floodplain near the airport, accentuates fluid dynamics and the power of the river. Like many of the firm's projects that engage hydrology, the park allows people to engage natural processes while they enjoy a stroll along the river.

Some cities are reclaiming entire deteriorating neighborhoods with the same end in mind. As a result, more and more examples are available of past mistakes being corrected while creating beautiful civic works that also serve important ecological functions. A project in the Near Northside area of Minneapolis is one such example where hydrology played a defining role. The vision for this project was developed in the mid-1990s through a neighborhood-city partnership and a project by the University of Minneapolis Design Center for American Urban Landscape (Figure 7.11). This area of the inner city had been built upon the former Bassett Creek and associated wetlands, and Sumner Fields, a 350-unit public housing project built there in 1938, suffered continuous structural problems. A 1996 University of Minnesota report attributed many of the ongoing problems to poor fill over

Figure 7.10 Guadalupe River Park in San Jose, California, designed by Hargreaves Associates.

wetland soils. That study proposed a major creek and wetland restoration project as the centerpiece of the planned redevelopment project, now called Heritage Park. "This system will function in multiple ways: provide a stream corridor with walking trails and wildlife habitat; create a distinct character for the surrounding neighborhood; treat storm flows for nonpoint source pollutants; and provide for a visible system that allows people to understand the water system functioning on the landscape surface."[21] This vision is now being implemented as a part of Heritage Park and of the new Bassett Creek Valley Masterplan.

This major investment by the city to restore Bassett Creek works hand in hand with land redevelopment to upgrade a blighted urban area. The city recognized that the parks and greenway component would be an important civic investment, one that would not only serve stormwater and ecological functions but also provide an important source of civic pride and identity. This greenway—composed of a linked series of stormwater gardens, wetlands, and a restored stream—is the centerpiece of this new neighborhood (Figure 7.12). Its location between the two armatures of Van White Memorial Boulevard ensures its very public, defining role in this neighborhood akin to Minneapolis's historic parkways conceived by planner H. W. S. Cleveland in the 1880s.

The Heritage Park project also achieves significant hydrological restoration. In its former state, this site was fraught with water-related structural problems on top of the typical pollution and volume problems of piped systems. The historic Bassett Creek that ran through this area was a low marshy area, underlain by deep silt and clay soils, near the confluence of the creek and the Mississippi River. The restored Bassett Creek is a modified creek and wetlands system, vastly different from its predevelopment parent but providing many similar functions. Ecologically, it will bring wetland and riparian habitat resources closer to the Mississippi River, although it does not complete the connection because downtown sits between the site and the river. The stormwater system will manage runoff volumes and filter pollution for an urban area of approximately 400 acres, 2.5 times the redevelopment area itself. The eventual goal is to extend the greenway across freeways and downtown to complete this linkage to the river.

Figure 7.11 Early diagram proposing the restoration of Bassett Creek in Minneapolis. (Source: Design Center for the American Urban Landscape, *Basset Creek Wetland Park*)

Figure 7.12 Heritage Park: the restored stream and stormwater gardens forming a linear green connection between two parks.

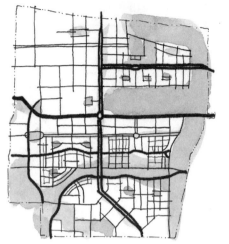

Figure 7.13 Stapleton: green and gray networks.

Linking across Scales

Perhaps the highest goal cities can aspire toward is to arrest the destruction of intact natural resources while incrementally working toward a long-term vision of a restored ecological structure within a system of interconnected greenways. Denver, Colorado, is taking advantage of major urban redevelopment projects to do just that. The Denver Metropolitan Area has several major interconnected greenways in various stages of planning and development, including the South Platte River, Cherry Creek, Sand Creek, and Westerly Creek. Once restored, these interconnected greenways will form a green network for the entire urban area.

Some of these greenways are still ideas on paper, while others—such as the South Platte River and Cherry Creek—are established green corridors. The Sand Creek Regional Greenway and Westerly Creek restorations are more recent, collaborative planning efforts that are getting out in front of major redevelopment efforts, the former Lowry Air Force Base and the former Stapleton Airport. These two ongoing redevelopment projects demonstrate how urban redevelopment provides opportunities to contribute to the metropolitan-scale green networks while also achieving major green infrastructure accomplishments at the neighborhood scale. Stapleton and the nearby Lowry development both include internal green corridors that restore streams and wetlands and very nearly connect with each other. Both developments also feature significant open space systems with major greenways along Westerly Creek and Sand Creek, respectively. Together, they will jump-start the Westerly Creek Greenway and the Sand Creek Regional Greenway as major armatures of restored landscape in east Denver. [22]

Stapleton is clearly the more ambitious project in terms of overall landscape restoration and a commitment to restoring local ecological functions (see the case study in Chapter 2). About 30 percent (1,116 acres) of Stapleton's 4,700 acres will be devoted to parks and open spaces; of that, roughly 75 percent will be in natural areas (Figure 7.13). During the airport days, Westerly Creek was a storm drainage pipe under the runways. Much of it has now been restored to a broad riparian corridor with a diverse ecosystem that includes streamside prairie, streamside forest, and wetlands (Figure 7.14). All of these ecosystems contribute

to on-site stormwater management,
slowing, infiltrating, and filtering
stormwater runoff from nearby developed areas. In fact, the urban
runoff from the developed portions
of Stapleton provide crucial clean
water resources for all of the restored
natural landscapes on the site.[23]

Figure 7.14 Stapleton: Westerly Creek
Greenway corridor.

Intimately connected to the
ecological and recreational purposes
of the greenway system are the
stormwater functions. Stapleton employs what might be called a
hybrid stormwater management system. Stormwater detention,
infiltration, and filtration are required on every development site,
including single-family homes. To aid builders, special stormwater management elements were designed for Stapleton to fit its
urban character and intensities. The development has some
neighborhood-scale stormwater parks, designed to detain and filter runoff. Much of the runoff, which flows from developed sites
and streets, is directed via underground pipes to large-scale facilities that are designed to resemble park features. These facilities
treat larger volumes of runoff before the water proceeds to the
bioswales, ponds, and wetlands in the greenways. Thus, the site
scale and the regional scale of stormwater management at Stapleton are naturally based approaches, while the conveyance system along the streets is a more conventional piped system. The
objective of the design approach is to fit stormwater management
into a dense urban context while also creating a new, healthy site
ecology that supports the restoration of major natural areas.

Whole Water Systems

The ideal urban stormwater management system would be one
that successfully mimics a landscape's natural hydrologic processes
while avoiding vast inputs of imported water to and outputs of
polluted water from the watershed. Its function would ensure that
the elements of the landscape's ecological structure—lakes, wetlands, streams, rivers, and upland natural areas—were not negatively affected by urbanization. To achieve such a system, all of

the urban landscape or the green infrastructure has to work toward this goal. The overriding goal of this approach to stormwater management would be "no net change" to a site's or a larger landscape's hydrology.

This concept comes out of the Low Impact Development (LID) movement, which is targeted at site-scaled development. The premise of LID is that through widespread micro-stormwater management, in which every site mimics its undeveloped hydrologic regime, the net result will be to more closely mimic the hydrology and the ecological and biological integrity of watersheds. LID is a process-oriented approach. The first step is to understand a site's natural, predevelopment hydrology. At the same time, at the scale of the subwatershed, watershed, and urban region, the most pressing hydrological problems should also be considered. For example, in the Pacific Northwest, damage to urban stream structure caused by high peak flows and warm waters is significantly affecting fish-bearing streams, whereas in arid regions and in areas of Florida, depletion of groundwater resources is a high-priority problem. Taken together, considering the site's natural hydrology along with the larger context informs the design strategies for on-site stormwater management. LID site designs are multifunctional, serving the basic user's needs in concert with stormwater management while also creating attractive urban landscapes. LID typically emphasizes, first and foremost, limiting areas of impervious surfaces and reducing the removal of natural land cover. Following that step, many naturally based strategies—including cisterns for storing water, biofiltration or infiltration areas (or "rain gardens"), swales, and French drains—are used in "trains" to maximize on-site management and minimize off-site drainage (Figure 7.4, 7.15). [24]

Of the numerous case studies of recent urban development or redevelopment featured in this book, Prairie Crossing in Gray's Lake, Illinois, provides the best example of this fully integrated approach to stormwater management (Figure 7.16). Prairie Crossing is a conservation community located in a rapidly suburbanizing area north of Chicago. Conceived to marry land conservation and a residential community, this development lies adjacent to the Liberty Prairie Preserve and was instigated by longtime residents who wanted to save the site from becoming a typical subdivision and add to the area's conservation lands. Of

Figure 7.15 Northwest 2nd Street, Seattle: a green street that includes stormwater detention and filtration along both sides.

the 677-acre site, 60 percent will remain open, as agricultural fields, restored prairie and wetlands, a lake, and parkland. This landscape is being restored to its historic presettlement prairie landscape, with parts also being converted to contemporary organic agriculture (Figure 7.17).[25]

Prairie Crossing's stormwater system was designed as an integral aspect of the site's ecosystem functions. For all but the high-density village center, runoff from the developed area runs overland through a four-step treatment train. From the streets and yards, stormwater travels through vegetated swales, which remove 20 to 25 percent of the key pollutants, such as suspended solids, nitrogen, phosphorous, and metals. From there, the water is directed via sheet flow over the restored prairie that surrounds housing. This further removes 60 to 85 percent of the key pollutants (Figure 7.18). After leaving the prairie, the water travels to stormwater wetlands for additional filtration and from there enters a constructed lake. This trip through the treatment train takes out 85 percent of phosphorous and nitrogen, 95 percent of metals, and 98 percent of suspended solids. Infiltration and evaporation along the way reduce stormwater volumes by 65 percent.[26] Concurrently, the extensive time spent traveling through swales and across the prairie allows much of the runoff to infiltrate into the ground, helping to maintain a balanced hydrology. Primary objectives of the system were to integrate stormwater management with the landscape restoration efforts so that the stormwater functioning was more or less invisible while at the same time serving the landscape restoration processes.

Coffee Creek Center, Heritage Park, Stapleton, and Prairie Crossing all demonstrate healthier, more natural approaches to managing urban water. These developments employ natural processes to mitigate the negative impacts of development on hydrology, yet none go all natural. Rather, they use adaptive approaches that vary in the extent to which they use technology and employ vegetation and soil to cleanse and infiltrate runoff. All put streams and wetlands center stage and make hydrological processes visible and tangible to the citizenry.

To restore the urban hydrologic balance, the management of water should occur across all scales of planning, design, and management—on individual sites, along neighborhood streets, in public open spaces, and through preservation and restoration of

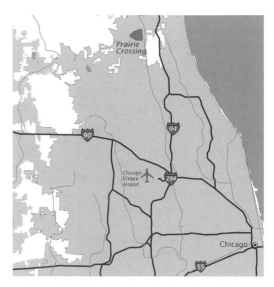
Figure 7.16 Prairie Crossing location diagram

Figure 7.17 Prairie Crossing land use plan shown in context

Figure 7.18 Prairie Crossing: the restored prairie serves as an important component of the stormwater management system.

regionwide lakes, rivers, and streams. Most fundamentally, the practice of capturing and discharging runoff from impervious surfaces to streams and rivers must be reversed. Every opportunity should be found to capture, filter, and infiltrate the city's natural water resource—rainfall—by forming a partnership between urban green spaces and water to structure the city and to sustain a healthy urban ecology. Managing hydrology might be seen as the "work" of urban landscapes.

Urban Water Strategies

- Protect and restore urban rivers, streams, lakes, and wetlands.
- Protect and augment natural hydrology across all scales of urban development.
- Keep urban pollutants out of natural waterways; capture and treat stormwater near its source.
- Use natural processes to filter stormwater.
- Make urban hydrology visible and tangible.
- Harvest rainwater for irrigation.

Chapter 8
Getting to Green Neighborhoods

Still lacking in most cities is a "vision" for the role of greenspaces; . . .
a greenstructure, which can be used as a resource.

A. Beer, T. Delshammar, and P. Schildwacht,
"A Changing Understanding of the Role of
Greenspace in High-density Housing"

If the form and spatial organization of cities are to be conceived
and constructed in partnership with nature and natural processes,
how close are we to understanding the spatial patterns that might
unlock this "green" urbanism as a matter of course rather than
exception? Have we found ways to merge patterns driven by
compact land use and transportation with environment-driven
patterns? Have we been able to leverage more and better civic
and economic benefits at the same time? And, perhaps most important, can we replicate those models that work well?

The record so far is mixed but not without promise. Clearly,
viable models of compact development have gained acceptance
and market share through the work of the Congress for the New
Urbanism (CNU) and the larger network of public and private
agencies loosely affiliated with the smart growth movement. These
groups have successfully elevated public awareness of the physical
attributes of compact development. They have advocated and promoted models and have provided crucial knowledge for professionals. The numbers of developments speak to the extent that
these principles have taken hold. CNU, for example, has grown
from a handful of members to more than 2,300 in about ten years.[1]
Development projects generated or influenced by principles of the
new urbanism have steadily increased in number and market share.
According to CNU, a neighborhood-scale "new urban" project is
one greater than 15 acres that features an interconnected network
of streets, a mix of housing types, at least one prominent central gathering space, and an overall emphasis on pedestrian-friendly character. *New Urban News* estimated in 2004 that 650 neighborhood-scale

projects based on new urbanism have been built, are under construction, or are planned in the United States alone. This represents a 37 percent increase over 2003 and an average increase of 28 percent for each of the previous seven years.[2]

Although they illustrate significant impact, these numbers still represent only a small fraction of the average of more than 1.6 million dwelling units constructed annually between1994 and 2004 in the United States. However, the principles and concepts that underlie them have been pervasive, influencing development patterns in many more ways than mere numbers of dwelling units may suggest. An influential body of planning and development policies, codes, and standards has directly influenced a significant percentage of development toward more compact patterns, whether or not they meet a "new urban" definition. Compact, transit-oriented development policies, codes, and standards adopted in the 1990s in Portland, Oregon, for example, reflect many of these priorities and characteristics. Their application and acceptance have precipitated a 3-dwelling-per-acre increase (from 5 to 8) in the average density of new housing development in roughly four years (1994 to 1998).[3] In addition, since Portland is widely watched as a laboratory for growth management innovation, some of the neighborhoods in which these dwellings are located may preview the positive impact of compact development models elsewhere.

While the principles and codes of compact development have gained influence, evidence of their anticipated environmental contributions has been slower to materialize. Evidence of the land conservation benefits is straightforward and compelling: more dense patterns consume less land. Unfortunately, the overwhelming majority of new housing developments are still located on exurban greenfield sites and thus consume rural land, albeit at a less voracious rate. Evidence of benefits to fossil fuel conservation and air quality that can be attributed to proximate mixed uses and pedestrian-oriented connective street networks generally support the promise of fewer, shorter automobile trips but can have only limited impact on trips outside the immediate neighborhood. For example, planners Yan Song and Gerrit-Jan Knaap note that although most new Portland neighborhoods are designed and built at higher densities and with well-connected, pedestrian-oriented streets, their context is often problematic. However promising these models of compact and livable neighborhoods are, they are often adjacent to automobile-oriented neighborhoods with poor pedestrian and bicycle networks. In these contexts, they are less effective as the building blocks of a whole and livable city or region. In the planners' own words: "Portland is winning the war on urban sprawl at the neighborhood scale, or at least appears to have won some important battles; but progress remains elusive at the regional scale."[4]

Fewer development models illustrate a comprehensive, replicable strategy for environmentally oriented development that includes issues of open space, water, and urban forests. Open space conservation (both natural and agricultural) figures prominently in many initiatives to manage growth and contain sprawl. Typically, the motivation is more to direct urban development away from particular natural assets, or to suppress the amount of growth overall, than it is to integrate the spatial pattern of growth with open space networks. Open space, it seems, is still perceived to be better off separated from development; because of the density of buildings and roads, more compact development patterns are perceived to compromise open space protection. Paradoxically, those who call for protection of open space often demand less dense, more distributed settlement patterns, believing that lower-density development will alleviate loss and fragmentation of open space overall.

The need for environmentally oriented development patterns has sharpened in recent years. Prodded by new water quality and habitat standards, many jurisdictions, such as Seattle and Portland, have pioneered development policies and regulations to protect their natural waterways. These policies and laws seek to protect the habitat values and spatial integrity of naturally occurring networks of waterways. As a result, the interaction of natural open space patterns and built patterns has dramatically elevated. A more environmentally beneficial pattern of urbanism would seek a contiguous open space and water network that linked surface water, groundwater, and built infrastructure into one integrated system. This would in turn influence transportation and land use patterns as well as the design of urban blocks and buildings within them.

Increasing public awareness of the integrity of natural networks and the potential of their integration with urban uses encourages a reconsideration of open space and the role it plays in urban design. Interconnected open space and water networks can significantly generate urban patterns. Indeed, design sensitive to open space and water has been intertwined in the literature of urban planning and design for some time. Long before smart growth and the new urbanism, many influential planners advocated open space and natural networks as organizing structures for development.[5] However reassuring that might seem on the surface, it is sobering to look back at past planning literature that sets out concepts very similar to what we call green networks and see that so little has been adopted or widely influential. With few exceptions, streets and transportation networks have been the primary influence on development patterns. Far less frequently, the spatial patterns of open space or ecological networks have generated a framework for urban form and development. Although natural areas, such as streams and wetlands, are being preserved within urban areas, this open space more often than not is residual.[6]

Truly smarter growth depends as much on the density and pattern of open space as it does on the location, density, and pattern of urban growth. Questions must be asked not only about where *not* to build but also about how much open space of what type, for what purpose, and in what relationship to buildings, yards, and streets there should be. Learning to layer an understanding of open space networks and environmental functions with these already complex, frequently competing urban priorities is, and will be, among the principal challenges to replicating "green" models of urban planning and design. Urban and environmental structures involve many elements and variables that reveal themselves in different ways at different spatial scales. Integrating them presents some unique conceptual and methodological challenges to the prevailing practices of urban planning and design. Meaningful linkages between the forces and patterns of nature and those of urban form must be more fully and wholly engaged. The gap we have to overcome is that environmental and ecological forces are rarely seen or weighed as equal, positive partners with land use and transportation.

Thinking, Seeing, and Knowing "Green"

Urban planning and design respond to the human constructs that identify significant systems and priorities of the city. Our challenge is, in part, to cultivate the habits of mind and to acquire the methods of working that help us think, see, and know "green" throughout the processes of urban planning and design. Elevating knowledge of natural ecosystems among those who make planning and design decisions is crucial. One means would be to reframe and sharpen the ways we represent the potential interactions, opportunities, and conflicts among the deep structures that relate urban and natural form in cities. A dual network strategy adapted from landscape ecology can enable the ecologically sound spatial organizations of urban areas to be considered. The green and gray networks we have proposed in this book as the two interacting urban frameworks can guide the pattern of development. Each reveals and disentangles a complex set of spaces and functions that increase in complexity as the scale of consideration becomes more refined. For example, at the scale of the metropolitan area, the green networks are the major river systems and large open space preserves, whereas at the neighborhood scale, the green networks are fine grained and include heterogeneous bits of nature, such as small patches of native vegetation and narrow green corridors. Acting together, coarse and fine grains form an integrated, functioning whole.

Nested Parcels, Districts, Neighborhoods, and Regions

The physical and functional connectivity of these structures across scales is the next important construct. Connectivity is needed both within a particular network and across the many networks of human, built, and natural systems in a region. Making these connections requires an understanding of a particular place in all its ecological, social, economic, transportation, and land use contexts and scales. For example, landscape ecologists typically study the ecological structure and processes of the larger landscape in which a city is situated. At the same time, bioregional ecological concerns as well as individual habitat types or populations must be considered. Understanding the larger context while working on a small site may reveal opportunities for a neighborhood's green infrastructure that may, in turn, shape a neighborhood's urban layout (and vice versa). Were such a cross-scaled approach more explicitly the norm, scales of planning and design would iteratively broaden or narrow in scope and focus from regions to sites and for scales in between (and back). Some structures and patterns would be more appropriately understood at a regional or metropolitan scale; others, at the city or neighborhood scale; and still others, at a site scale. Understanding the whole can amplify the layers and potential points of connection and interdependence across scales. For example, understood in a larger context, a remnant wetland or a fragment of stream corridor provides an opportunity to make habitat connections when it coincides with parallel opportunities to link to nearby parks, schools, or bikeways.

Integrating Compact Green and Gray: Vancouver, British Columbia

New neighborhoods are the building blocks of cities. When developed correctly, multiple neighborhoods have the potential to build healthy regions. Vancouver, British Columbia, is one city making progress toward the integration of compact development and green infrastructure at the neighborhood scale as part of a regionwide vision. Already a relatively compact city, Vancouver accommodates approximately 25 percent of its regional population and 35 percent of its jobs in about 4 percent of its land area. It is also one of very few large metropolitan areas in North America that are not bisected by a major freeway; not coincidentally, it is frequently cited as one of the most livable cities in the world.

For a longer time, and with greater enthusiasm and persistence than many other cities, Vancouver has encouraged people to live in and near the downtown. Since the 1980s, about 8 million square feet of excess commercial (office) capacity has been converted to residential capacity and related services near central city jobs. Old rail yards and industrial areas were earmarked for housing, and an aggressive planning effort, the "Living First" urban design strategy, was implemented.[7] The goal of this strategy has been to create urban communities that are more sustainable environmentally, socially, and economically. An underlying theme has been to enable an urban lifestyle that is more attractive than a suburban one, which involves, as one aspect, creating attractive counterparts to the single-family suburban dwelling. For example, to attract families with children, most new developments include row housing or stacked townhouses with direct connections to the ground and outdoor areas. Neighborhoods also are designed to ensure access to a rich palette of convenient urban experiences in neighborhoods that are as safe and secure as those of the suburbs. The result has been a development pattern that has grown increasingly dense while at the same time adding significant new public open space and amenities in the central city.

For its Living First strategy, Vancouver has developed its own structuring and organizing principles of urban design:

- Give priority to transit, cycle, and pedestrian (and limit commuter car) access in the downtown.
- Develop complete neighborhoods at a pedestrian scale—a mix of mutually supportive uses and activities focused on a commercial high street and other amenities (parks, schools, day cares, community centers, and so forth).
- Provide a rich, diverse mix of housing types and tenures.
- Extend the fabric, patterns, and character of the existing city into adjacent new development.
- Ensure that open space and green linkages are paramount and that waterfront edges are always public.

Also notable in Vancouver is an active partnership among planning, design, and development professionals that has been necessary to achieve these principles. The city has worked with the professional community to set standards that are workable on both sides. For example, the traditional relationships among the street, the sidewalk, and the building facade, and between buildings themselves, are crucial to making higher densities work. Design guidelines, enabled by zoning, set a palette of thin high-rise towers with small footprints. The high-rises are screened from pedestrians by lower street-oriented uses with shops, restaurants, grocery stores, and other services. The towers disappear behind a pedestrian-scale streetscape. Almost all parking is underground, except for short-term curbside spaces on local streets. In turn, higher allowable densities generate sufficient value to encourage developers to use higher-quality materials and create on-site amenities.

The strategy has been successful. The central city has added about 20,000 people since the late 1980s. At current rates of growth, the central city population will more than double, to 90,000, by 2015. The ultimate planned residential capacity of about 110,000 people is being approached at a rate faster than anyone anticipated. This represents a land savings of approximately 5,000 to 7,000 acres if that same population had moved to suburban areas at typical densities. At the same time, more than 65 acres of new parks have been added to the downtown, and the public waterfront promenade has expanded to more than 20 kilometers in the past decade.[8]

South East False Creek

> There are some fundamental changes going on. It's increasingly possible to live in Vancouver without a motor vehicle.
>
>   C. Johnson, "Fewer Vehicles on Road as People Opt for Transit"

After land conservation, one frequently cited environmental benefit of compact development is that people drive less. While evidence has been mixed in other cities, Vancouver's experience offers early, unambiguous evidence that, at least under some circumstances, people will choose walking and transit over automobiles. About 28 percent of Vancouver's downtown residents walk to work, and about 42 percent of other city residents coming downtown do so by public transit. At the same time, the rate of car ownership in the city has declined for the first time after a decade of steady increases.[9] Other data support the interpretation that Vancouver's urban transportation mode mix has now tipped toward more sustainable alternatives. Between 1994 and 1999, daily automobile movements in the downtown decreased by 13 percent while pedestrian movements increased by 55 percent. In fact, the flow of automobiles may have reversed, since there is now a measurable net outflow of cars from the downtown to other areas of the city.

> SEFC is envisioned as a community in which people live, work, play and learn in a neighborhood that has been designed to maintain and

balance the highest possible levels of social equity, livability, ecological
health and economic prosperity, so as to support their choices to live in
a sustainable manner.

City of Vancouver, "South East False Creek Policy Statement"

Adjacent to downtown Vancouver, South East False Creek
(SEFC) is the newest community planned for approximately 80
acres of a former inner-city industrial area, the last remaining waterfront in the False Creek basin (Figure 8.1). Since the late
1800s, the area has accommodated heavy industrial and transportation land uses, including sawmills, foundries, shipbuilding,
metalworking, salt distribution, warehousing, and public works
facilities. As a result of the major shift in land use priorities that
had been unfolding since the 1970s, first at False Creek South
and later at False Creek North, industrial uses had all but aban-
doned the area by the 1990s. As it had with many other under-
utilized commercial and industrial areas in the downtown, the
City released SEFC from the industrial land base in 1995.

Notably, the timing of this conversion parallels an increasing
public interest and political will on the part of the City to advance the cause of environmental quality in the region. "Sustainable development" was added to the planning and urban design
mandate that would shape SEFC. Where prior central city planning had concentrated on, and substantially achieved, livable
models of compact development, SEFC would do this in addition to elevating an emerging environmental agenda. The overall intent was to create a dense, mixed-use urban neighborhood
with three- to twelve-story buildings while concurrently reducing energy and resource consumption as well as waste and pollution generation (Figure 8.2). When completed, a diverse mix
of approximately 5,000 dwelling types will create three neighborhoods that derive their form from the historic pattern of the
adjacent neighborhood.

These neighborhoods are to be integrated with a network of
streets, parks, and public spaces that organizes the development
pattern of the site (Figure 8.3). Streets, paths, and transit will also
connect SEFC to adjacent areas and regional systems. Integrating
consideration of environmental performance in very early stages
of planning and design has profoundly affected the proposed

Figure 8.1 South East False Creek: aerial view
of site (shaded) looking toward downtown
and the north-shore mountains, City of
Vancouver, *Draft ODP By-law for South East
False Creek*)

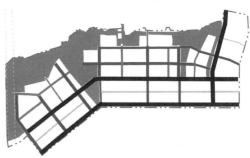

Figure 8.2 South East False Creek: green and
gray networks

Figure 8.3 South East False Creek: (a) diagram of major open spaces, (b) diagram of the three neighborhoods, and (c) diagram of major transportation routes. (Source: Via Architecture et al., *South East False Creek Official Development Plan*)

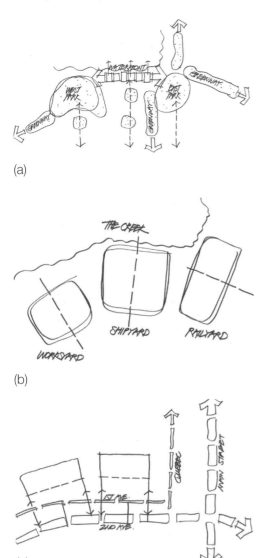

(a)

(b)

(c)

development for the better. The current concept plan proposes a very dense and urban mix of approximately 5,000 market, low end of market, and nonmarket (subsidized) dwelling units that are well served by commercial, educational, cultural, and recreational services at an average floor-space ratio of 3.5 and a gross density of about 60 dwellings per acre.[10]

Approximately 26 acres of parks and public open spaces will form a green infrastructure that supports stormwater management, urban agriculture, and other ecological functions alongside traditional recreation and open space functions. With this public green network in place, private development can be designed to leverage that investment, enabling more sustainable strategies at the urban block, parcel, and building scales, such as green roofs, stormwater infiltration and harvesting, urban agriculture, and recycling.

Impressive goals for environmental performance are within reach for South East False Creek. All of the dwellings can be located within 1,200 feet of basic shopping, personal services, and transit choices (bus, rapid transit, streetcar, and pedestrian ferries), and 60 percent of all daily trips can be by modes other than automobile. Parking requirements can be reduced, and 100 percent of the streets can be designed to favor walking, cycling, and transit over private automobiles. Water use per capita can be reduced to 50 percent of the regional average, and 12.5 percent of the produce consumed by residents can be grown on-site in public open spaces or private green roofs. About 60 percent of the site can effectively be "pervious," with stormwater being managed through an on-site infiltration and conveyance network. In the public domain, road widths have been reduced, and all curbs, gutters, and storm sewers can be eliminated. About 60 percent of all open space and 80 percent of the foreshore can have significant habitat value. Targets include a range of habitats for at least thirty species of birds.[11]

The first built results are anticipated with the construction of the 2010 Winter Olympic Village in 2006. With this development, the city will add another benchmark to what Welsh urban design author and critic John Punter considers Vancouver's justifiable "claim to be a compact, proto-sustainable city with a livable downtown surrounded by a series of high-density, mixed use residential areas, whose residents need not commute by car but can walk, cycle or use transit for many of their urban trips."[12] The real legacy, however, will be more systemic in that it will bring replicable models of urban planning and design to the region as well as to worldwide cities. On that point, Punter adapts Jonathan Barnett's phrase "urban design as public policy" to capture the unusual convergence of place, economy, and politics that has enabled this reformation of the development pattern since the 1970s.[13]

It is a theme that resonates with local experience. Former Vancouver city councilor and urban planning consultant Gordon Price directly participated in the political processes that created False Creek North and SEFC. Reflection on that experience has inspired him to summarize six interdependent conditions for achieving compact, mixed-use communities that are clean, green, and safe. First and foremost is a *community that chooses* (politically and publicly) to contain growth, to value environment, and to value livability. Second is a *regional framework,* a larger-scale strategy for coordinated planning of the land use, transportation, and environmental infrastructure. Third and fourth are constituencies of informed *market providers,* the entrepreneurs, professionals, and *bankers* capable of initiating, designing, financing, and implementing compact and green development patterns. Fifth is a parallel and equally robust constituency of educated, astute, and motivated *market consumers*—voters, homeowners, and renters who will choose to live in these communities. Sixth is a *reliable political, regulatory, and legal system*—the city councils, planning commissions, regulators, and adjudication processes that facilitate translation of policy into pattern and, finally, into action on the ground.

Reflections on Green Neighborhoods

So, what do South East False Creek and the other case studies that we explore in this book tell us about green neighborhoods? What are their essential attributes? Green neighborhoods are first and foremost neighborhoods, those areas of a city in which people say they live, work, learn, or play. They have spatial attributes defined by domain and edges, and are roughly the distance that one can walk to services or to a transit stop. Typically that represents a land area of roughly 125 to 500 acres. On top of that, they are "green," that is, they are explicitly designed to conserve and

protect land, water, and air. The best ones go even further and
contribute to a healthy urban ecosystem with artful design and the
integration of green networks, green streets, green buildings, and
green infrastructure that merge urban functions with natural
processes. These physical patterns must be complemented by a
public policy and political framework that value environment and
enable implementation.

Distinguishing characteristics include:

• Neighborhoods are areas of a city in which people say they
live, work, learn, or play; neighborhoods have spatial attributes of domain and edge.
• The term "neighborhood" has come to be defined as the distance that one can walk to services or to a transit stop (between five and ten minutes, or a quarter to a half mile for
most people) and represents a land area of roughly 125 to 500
acres.

Green neighborhoods have the following characteristics.

Green Networks

• A vision for protecting, restoring, and interconnecting urban
ecological structure
• Multifunctional green networks at every planning scale—the
metropolitan area, the city, and the neighborhood
• A research community and citizenry that understand the
city's ecosystem
• Landscape restoration that repairs fragmented ecological
structure
• Natural processes visibly integrated in the design of urban
landscapes

Gray Networks

• Accessible, connective street networks
• Excellent accessibility and connectivity for pedestrians and
bicycles
• Street networks adapted to site conditions and avoiding sen-
sitive natural resources

- Green streets that manage their own stormwater and maximize tree canopy cover
- Shorter, narrower, less impervious streets
- Beautiful, tree-lined streets and paths

Gray Fabric

- Compact and complete neighborhoods with residential densities of 12 to 30 persons per acre in low-rise areas and 75 to 100 persons per acre in mid- to high-rise areas
- A diverse, pedestrian-oriented neighborhood service center within walking distance of the majority of dwellings
- Schools, churches, parks, and squares within walking distance of most dwellings
- A fine-grained mix of residential and smaller-scale commercial uses that surrounds the service center
- A diverse mix of housing types and densities that serves a broad cross section of households
- Ground-oriented family housing at many densities

Green Fabric

- A healthy, sustainable urban forest that contributes to civic beauty and to a healthy urban ecosystem
- Urban forest as a keystone component of green networks
- Preserved remnant forests and mature trees
- An urban forest canopy covering 40 percent of the neighborhood area
- Memorable, distinctive, tree-covered spaces
- Streets trees selected for long-term contributions to the urban forest

Urban Water

- Protected and restored urban rivers, streams, lakes, and wetlands
- Protected and augmented natural hydrology across all scales of urban development
- Stormwater runoff captured and treated close to its source
- Natural processes to filter stormwater
- Visible and tangible urban hydrology

- Treatment trains—linked stormwater management strategies—throughout the neighborhood
- Stormwater harvested for irrigation

Getting to Green

- A community that chooses growth management, environmental quality, and livability
- A regional framework that coordinates environmental, transportation, and infrastructure resources
- Market providers who initiate, design, and build green development
- Financial service providers who value and finance green development
- Market consumers who understand and appreciate the value of green development
- Reliable political, regulatory, and legal systems that support, implement, and enforce green development policies and laws

Notes

Preface

1. Carson, *Silent Spring;* Ehrlich, *The Population Bomb;* Club of Rome, *The Limits of Growth.*
2. McHarg, *Design with Nature;* Olgyay, *Design with Climate.*
3. Hough, *City Form and Natural Process;* Spirn, *The Granite Garden.*
4. Morrish, *Summary Report;* Condon, *Sustainable Urban Landscapes.*

Introduction

1. Hobbs, Stoops, and U.S. Bureau of the Census, *U.S. Bureau of the Census, Census 2000 Special Reports, Series CENSR-4.*
2. Hobbs, Stoops, and U.S. Bureau of the Census, *U.S. Bureau of the Census, Census 2000 Special Reports, Series CENSR-4.*
3. National Association of Home Builders, *Housing Facts, Figures and Trends 2001.*
4. National Association of Home Builders, *Housing Facts, Figures and Trends 2001.*
5. U.S. Environmental Protection Agency, *Our Built and Natural Environments.*
6. B. Katz and Lang, eds., *Redefining Urban and Suburban America.*
7. U.S. Bureau of the Census, "Table B-1."
8. Read, "'More Bedrooms than People to Sleep in Them' in Richer Areas."
9. Frank, Engelke, and Schmid, *Health and Community Design.*
10. Dunham-Jones, "Seventy-Five Percent."
11. Gause et al., *Great Planned Communities.*
12. Podobnik, "The Social and Environmental Achievements of New Urbanism."
13. Robert Thayer, personal communication, July 1991; Francis, *Village Homes.*
14. Francis, *Village Homes.*
15. Francis, *Village Homes.*

1. Green Neighborhoods

1. Moughtin, *Urban Design,* p. 117.
2. Moughtin, *Urban Design.*
3. Perry, "The Neighborhood Unit."

4. U.S. Federal Housing Administration, *Planning Profitable Neighborhoods.*

5. Girling and Helphand, *Yard, Street, Park.*

6. Andres Duany's and Elizabeth Plater-Zyberk's "Thirteen Points of Traditional Neighborhood Development," as presented in Steuteville, "The New Urbanism."

7. Congress for the New Urbanism, *Charter of the New Urbanism.*

8. Lynch, *A Theory of Good City Form.*

9. Stein, *Toward New Towns for America.*

10. Calthorpe, *The Next American Metropolis.*

3. Green Networks

1. Ferguson, *Stormwater Infiltration;* Hough, *Cities and Natural Process;* Wenk, "Toward an Inclusive Concept of Infrastructure."

2. Platt, Rowntree, and Muick, eds., *The Ecological City;* Cook, "Landscape Structure Indices for Assessing Urban Ecological Networks."

3. President's Council on Sustainable Development, *Towards a Sustainable America,* p. 64.

4. U.S. Department of Agriculture Forest Service, *An Ecosystem Approach to Urban and Community Forestry;* Wolf, "From Tree to Forest."

5. Benedict and McMahon, "Green Infrastructure," p. 12.

6. Benedict and McMahon, "Green Infrastructure," p. 12.

7. Beatley, *Green Urbanism.*

8. Beatley, *Green Urbanism.*

9. Heckscher and Robinson, *Open Spaces.*

10. Heckscher and Robinson, *Open Spaces.*

11. President's Commission on Americans Outdoors, *Americans Outdoors.*

12. Little, *Greenways for America.*

13. Benfield, Raimi, and Chen, *Once There Were Greenfields;* Renner and Sheehan, *Vital Signs 2003;* Noss, "Conservation of Biodiversity on Western Rangelands"; U.S. Environmental Protection Agency, *Our Built and Natural Environments.*

14. Benfield, Raimi, and Chen, *Once There Were Greenfields.*

15. Hulse and Baker, eds., *Willamette River Basin Planning Atlas.*

16. Smith and Hellmund, *Ecology of Greenways.*

17. Hulse and Baker, eds., *Willamette River Basin Planning Atlas.*

18. B. Johnson and Hill, *Ecology and Design,* p. 13.

19. Beatley, *Green Urbanism,* p. 6.

20. Beatley, *Green Urbanism,* p. 5.

21. Forman and Godron, *Landscape Ecology.*

22. Forman and Godron, *Landscape Ecology;* Dramstad, Olson, and Forman, *Landscape Ecology Principles.*

23. Forman and Godron, *Landscape Ecology;* Dramstad, Olson, and Forman, *Landscape Ecology Principles.*

24. Forman, "The Missing Catalyst."

25. Peck, *Planning for Biodiversity.*

26. Peck, *Planning for Biodiversity.*

27. Forman, "The Missing Catalyst"; Hough, "Looking beneath the Surface."

28. Hough, "Looking beneath the Surface."

29. Smith and Hellmund, *Ecology of Greenways;* Peck, *Planning for Biodiversity.*

30. Poracsky and Houck, "The Metropolitan Portland Urban Natural Resource Program."

31. Metro, *Metro's Open Spaces Land Acquisition Report to Citizens.*

32. Metro, *Metro's Open Spaces Land Acquisition Report to Citizens.*

33. Forman, "The Missing Catalyst."

34. Wenk, "Toward an Inclusive Concept of Infrastructure."

35. City of Surrey et al., *East Clayton Neighbourhood Concept Plan.*

36. City of Surrey et al., *East Clayton Neighbourhood Concept Plan.*

37. Greater Vancouver Regional District, *Creating Greater Vancouver's Green Zone;* Greater Vancouver Regional District, *Livable Region Strategic Plan.*

4. Gray Networks

1. Southworth and Ben-Joseph, "Streets and the Shaping of Suburbia."

2. Holtzclaw, "Explaining Urban Density and Travel Impacts on Auto Use"; S. L. Handy, "Understanding the Link between Urban Form and Non-work Travel Behavior."

3. U.S. Department of Transportation, *National Personal Transportation Survey.*

4. 1000 Friends of Oregon, *Making the Connections.*

5. Kessler and Schroeer, *Meeting Mobility and Air Quality Goals.*

6. Hu and Young, *Summary of Travel Trends.*

7. U.S. Department of Transportation, *National Personal Transportation Survey,* p. 4-2.

8. Northwest Environment Watch, "Fueling Up."

9. S. L. Handy, "Understanding the Link between Urban Form and Non-work Travel Behavior"; Northwest Environment Watch, "Sprawl and Smart Growth in Greater Vancouver."

10. Nelessen, *Visions for a New American Dream;* Ewing, *Best Development Practices;* Congress for the New Urbanism, *Charter of the New Urbanism.*

11. S. L. Handy, "Understanding the Link between Urban Form and Non-work Travel Behavior"; Lund, "Testing the Claims of New Urbanism Local Access, Pedestrian Travel and Neighboring Behaviors."

12. Moudon, *Effects of Site Design on Pedestrian Travel in Mixed-use, Medium-density Environments.*

13. S. L. Handy, "Understanding the Link between Urban Form and Non-work Travel Behavior"; Talen, "Pedestrian Access as a Measure of Urban Quality."

14. Ewing, *Best Development Practices;* Southworth and Ben-Joseph, *Streets and the Shaping of Towns and Cities.*

15. Ewing, *Best Development Practices.*

16. Ewing, *Transportation and Land Use Innovations.*

17. 1000 Friends of Oregon, *The Pedestrian Environment.*

18. Ewing, *Transportation and Land Use Innovations;* Talen, "Pedestrian Access as a Measure of Urban Quality."

19. Landis et al., *Modeling the Roadside Environment.*

20. Ewing, *Best Development Practices;* Ewing, *Transportation and Land Use Innovations.*

21. Ewing, *Best Development Practices.*

22. Moudon, "The Evolution of Common Twentieth Century Residential Forms."

23. Southworth and Ben-Joseph, *Streets and the Shaping of Towns and Cities.*

24. Stein, *Toward New Towns for America.*

25. Girling and Helphand, *Yard, Street, Park;* S. Handy, Brown, and Butler, "Planning for Street Connectivity."

26. S. Handy, Brown, and Butler, "Planning for Street Connectivity"; Moudon, *Effects of Site Design on Pedestrian Travel in Mixed-use, Medium-density Environments.*

27. Ben-Joseph, *Livability and Safety of Suburban Street Patterns.*

28. Southworth and Ben-Joseph, "Streets and the Shaping of Suburbia."

29. Center for Watershed Protection, *Better Site Design;* Girling and Kellett, "Comparing Stormwater Impacts and Costs on Three Neighborhood Plan Types."

30. Ewing, *Best Development Practices;* Southworth and Ben-Joseph, *Streets and the Shaping of Towns and Cities.*

31. Girling and Helphand, *Yard, Street, Park.*

32. Kellett, *Measuring Infrastructure in New Community Development.*

33. U.S. Environmental Protection Agency, "Non-point Source News Notes #44."

34. Schueler, Center for Watershed Protection, and Metropolitan Washington Council of Governments, *Site Planning for Urban Stream Protection;* Girling and Kellett, "Comparing Stormwater Impacts and Costs on Three Neighborhood Plan Types."

35. Gangnes, "Seattle's Green Streets Ripe for Modernization."

36. Metro, *Green Streets.*

37. Metro, *Green Streets.*

38. Southworth and Ben-Joseph, "Streets and the Shaping of Suburbia."

39. Atkins, "Traffic Calming."

40. American Society of Civil Engineers, National Association of Home Builders, and Urban Land Institute, *Residential Streets;* American Association of State Highway and Transportation Officials, *A Policy on Geometric Design of Highways and Streets.*

41. Southworth, "Walkable Suburbs?"

42. Swift, *Residential Street Typology and Injury Accident Frequency.*

43. Ewing, *Best Development Practices;* Neighborhoods Streets Project Stakeholders, *Neighborhood Street Design Guidelines.*

44. American Association of State Highway and Transportation Officials, *A Policy on Geometric Design of Highways and Streets.*

45. Schueler, Center for Watershed Protection, and Metropolitan Washington Council of Governments, *Site Planning for Urban Stream Protection*.

46. Strang, "Infrastructure as Landscape."

47. Thayer, "Increasingly Invisible Infrastructure," p. 136.

48. Fisher, "From the Water's Edge (San Francisco)."

49. Freeman, "Above the Cut."

50. Lecesse, "A Point Well Taken."

51. Rosenberg, "Public Works and Public Space," p. 101.

52. A. B. Jacobs, *Great Streets*, p. 312.

53. City of Minneapolis, *Minneapolis near Northside: Master Plan*.

54. Brand, "The End of the Runway."

55. Stapleton Redevelopment Foundation, *Stapleton Development Plan;* Gause et al., *Great Planned Communities*.

5. Gray Fabric

1. Ecological Footprint Quiz, http://www.ecofoot.org.

2. P. Katz, *The New Urbanism;* Congress for the New Urbanism, *Charter of the New Urbanism*.

3. 1000 Friends of Oregon, *Making the Connections;* Jack Faucett Associates and Sierra Research, "Background Information for Land Use SIP Policy"; Crane, *The Impacts of Urban Form on Travel*.

4. Holtzclaw, "Explaining Urban Denisty and Travel Impacts on Auto Use."

5. 1000 Friends of Oregon, *The Pedestrian Environment;* S. L. Handy, "Understanding the Link between Urban Form and Non-work Travel Behavior"; 1000 Friends of Oregon, *Making the Connections*.

6. Cervero and Radisch, *Travel Choices in Pedestrian Versus Automobile Oriented Neighborhoods*.

7. Frank and Pivo, "Impacts of Mixed Use and Density..."

8. Institute of Transportation Engineers, *ITE Trip Generation Handbook*.

9. Northwest Environment Watch, *This Place on Earth 2002;* Northwest Environment Watch, "Sprawl and Smart Growth in Greater Seattle-Tacoma"; Northwest Environment Watch, "Sprawl and Smart Growth in Metropolitan Portland"; Northwest Environment Watch, "Portland's 'Smart Growth' Pays Off, Clark County Comparison Shows"; Northwest Environment Watch, "Sprawl and Smart Growth in Greater Vancouver"; Northwest Environment Watch, "Fueling Up."

10. Beatley, *Green Urbanism;* Northwest Environment Watch, *Cascadia Scorecard;* Smart Growth Network, "Principles of Smart Growth."

11. Northwest Environment Watch, *Cascadia Scorecard*.

12. Beatley, *Green Urbanism;* Statistics Canada, "Central Area Growth Statistics."

13. Steuteville, ed., *New Urbanism*.

14. Northwest Environment Watch, *Cascadia Scorecard*.

15. Calthorpe, *The Next American Metropolis*.

16. Steuteville, ed., *New Urbanism*.

17. Newman, *Community of Interest;* Marcus and Sarkissian, *Housing as if People Mattered.*

18. Statistics Canada, "Kitsilano."

19. Barton, Grant, and Guise, *Shaping Neighbourhoods.*

20. Calthorpe, *The Next American Metropolis.*

21. Steuteville, ed., *New Urbanism.*

22. Greater Vancouver Regional District, *Livable Region Strategic Plan.*

23. De Chiara, Panero, and Zelnik, *Time-saver Standards for Housing and Residential Development;* Steuteville, ed., *New Urbanism.*

24. Calthorpe, "The Urban Network."

25. Lynch and Hack, *Site Planning.*

26. Metro, "2040 Growth Concept."

27. Bohl, *Place Making.*

28. Podobnik, "The Social and Environmental Achievements of New Urbanism."

29. Calthorpe, *The Next American Metropolis.*

30. Katz, *The New Urbanism;* Beatley, *Green Urbanism;* Statistics Canada, "Central Area Growth Statistics"; S. A. Johnson and Lang, "Changing the Grid."

31. Smart Growth Network, *Getting to Smart Growth II.*

32. Bohl, *Place Making.*

33. Podobnik, "The Social and Environmental Achievements of New Urbanism."

6. Green Fabric

1. Grey and Deneke, *Urban Forestry;* TreePeople, *Second Nature.*

2. U.S. Department of Agriculture Forest Service, *An Ecosystem Approach to Urban and Community Forestry.*

3. Wackernagel and Rees, *Our Ecological Footprint.*

4. American Forests, *Regional Ecosystem Analysis Puget Sound Metropolitan Area.*

5. American Forests, *Regional Ecosystem Analysis for the Willamette/Lower Columbia Region.*

6. R. Kaplan, "The Green Experience."

7. Kaplan and Kaplan, *The Experience of Nature;* Ulrich, "The Role of Trees in Human Well-being and Health"; S. Kaplan, "The Restorative Environment"; Ulrich, "Benefits of Urban Greening for Human Well-being"; R. Kaplan, "The Nature of the View from Home."

8. Appleyard, "Urban Trees, Urban Forests."

9. Nowak, Crane, and Dwyer, "Compensatory Value of Urban Trees in the United States."

10. U.S. Environmental Protection Agency, *Cooling Our Communities.*

11. McPherson, "Atmospheric Carbon Dioxide Reduction by Sacramento's Urban Forest."

12. U.S. Environmental Protection Agency, *Cooling Our Communities.*

13. Spirn, *The Granite Garden.*

14. U.S. Environmental Protection Agency, *Cooling Our Communities.*

15. Nowak and Dwyer, "Understanding the Benefits and Costs of Urban Forest Ecosystems."

16. Dramstad, Olson, and Forman, *Landscape Ecology Principles.*

17. U.S. Department of Agriculture Forest Service, *An Ecosystem Approach to Urban and Community Forestry.*; Wolf, "From Tree to Forest."

18. Hough, *Cities and Natural Process.*

19. Xiao et al., "Rainfall Interception by Sacramento's Urban Forest"; Nowak and Dwyer, "Understanding the Benefits and Costs of Urban Forest Ecosystems."

20. Dwyer, McPherson, et al., "Assessing the Benefits and Costs of the Urban Forest."

21. Xiao et al., "Rainfall Interception by Sacramento's Urban Forest."

22. Girling and Lamb, "Comparing Alternative Urban Forestry Scenarios for the Royal Avenue Specific Plan in Eugene, OR."

23. Great Plains/Rocky Mountain Hazardous Substance Research Center, "Phytoremediation."

24. Moll and Ebenreck, eds., *Shading Our Cities.*

25. American Forests, *Regional Ecosystem Analysis Puget Sound Metropolitan Area;* American Forests, *Regional Ecosystem Analysis for the Willamette/Lower Columbia Region.*

26. Tunney, "Innovative Stormwater Design."

27. Metro, *Green Streets; Trees for Green Streets.*

28. Costa Pacific Homes, "Villebois to Feature Cutting Edge Rainwater Management and 'Green' Development Practices."

29. David Aulwes of Walker Macy, personal communication, February 17, 2004.

30. Alpha Engineering Inc. et al., *Villebois,* vol. 4.

31. Alpha Engineering Inc. et al., *Villebois,* vol. 4.

32. A. B. Jacobs, *Great Streets.*

33. A. B. Jacobs, *Great Streets.*

34. Arnold, *Trees in Urban Design.*

35. Arnold, *Trees in Urban Design.*

36. A. B. Jacobs, *Great Streets;* Strom, "Urban and Community Forestry."

37. Ellis, "The Spatial Structure of Streets."

38. Girling and Helphand, *Yard, Street, Park;* A. B. Jacobs, *Great Streets.*

39. Schuyler et al., eds., *The Papers of Frederick Law Olmsted,* vol. 6, p. 286.

40. Arnold, *Trees in Urban Design;* A. B. Jacobs, *Great Streets.*

41. Costa Pacific Homes, "Villebois to Feature Cutting Edge Rainwater Management and 'Green' Development Practices."

42. Walker Macy et al., *Villebois,* vol. 4.

43. David Aulwes, personal communication, February 17, 2004.

44. City of Wilsonville, "Tree Preservation and Protection"; Walker Macy et al., *Villebois,* vol. 4.

45. Walker Macy et al., *Villebois,* vol. 4.

7. Urban Water

1. Loizeaux–Bennett, "Stormwater and Nonpoint-source Runoff."
2. Water Environment Federation and American Society of Civil Engineers, *Urban Runoff Quality Management.*
3. Ferguson, *Stormwater Infiltration.*
4. Stiffler and McClure, "Our Troubled Sound."
5. U.S. Environmental Protection Agency, "Menu of B.M.P.s."
6. Brinckman, "The Endangered Species Listings."
7. Metro, "Title 3 Model Ordinance."
8. Ferguson, *Introduction to Stormwater;* Water Environment Federation and American Society of Civil Engineers, *Urban Runoff Quality Management.*
9. Spirn, *The Granite Garden,* p. 167; Hough, *City Form and Natural Process.*
10. Tom Richman & Associates et al., *Start at the Source;* Water Environment Federation and American Society of Civil Engineers, *Urban Runoff Quality Management.*
11. For more information on low-impact development, see http://www.lowimpactdevelopment.org. For more on infiltration stormwater systems, see Tom Richman & Associates et al., *Start at the Source.*
12. Spirn, *The Granite Garden;* Smith and Hellmund, *Ecology of Greenways;* Girling and Helphand, *Yard, Street, Park.*
13. Springgate and Hoesterey, "Bellevue, Washington"; Girling and Helphand, "Retrofitting Suburbia."
14. Quoted in Farnsworth, "Re-imaging the Future."
15. Gause et al., *Great Planned Communities;* Kalkbrenner, Wolfe, and J. F. New and Associates Inc., "Coffee Creek Center."
16. Dreiseitl, Grau, and Ludwig, eds., *Waterscapes.* http://www.coffeecreekcenter.com.
17. Rinne, "Hydroscape/Cityscape."
18. Dreiseitl, Grau, and Ludwig, eds., *Waterscapes,* p. 9.
19. Wenk, "Toward an Inclusive Concept of Infrastructure," p. 176.
20. Strutin, "Two Parks That Quiet the Storm."
21. City of Minneapolis, *Minneapolis New North Side Plan,* p. 27.
22. Sand Creek Regional Greenway, *Sand Creek Regional Greenway;* City of Denver, *Game Plan.*
23. *Stapleton Parks and Recreation Master Plan.*
24. Prince George's County, *Low-impact Development.* See also http://www.lowimpactdevelopment.org.
25. Bradford, Herron, and Greet, "Hometowns"; Kane, "Prairie Flower."
26. Apfelbaum et al., "The Prairie Crossing Project."

8. Getting to Green Neighborhoods

1. For more information about the Congress for the New Urbanism, see

http://www.cnu.org.

2. Steuteville, "New Neighborhoods Make Big Gains."

3. Squires, ed., *Urban Sprawl.*

4. Song and Knapp, "Measuring Urban Form," p. 223.

5. Heckscher and Robinson, *Open Spaces;* Whyte, *The Last Landscape.*

6. Erickson, "Can Open Space Shape Development?"

7. Beasley, "'Living First' in Downtown Vancouver."

9. C. Johnson, "Fewer Vehicles on Road as People Opt for Transit."

10. City of Vancouver, *Draft ODP By-law for South East False Creek.*

11. reSource Rethinking Building Inc. et al., *Merge Consultancy Report for South East False Creek.*

12. Punter, *The Vancouver Achievement,* p. 346.

13. Punter, *The Vancouver Achievement.*

Bibliography

1000 Friends of Oregon. *Making the Connections: A Summary of the LUTRAQ Project: Integrating Land-Use and Transportation Planning for Livable Communities.* Portland: 1000 Friends of Oregon, 1997.

————. *The Pedestrian Environment.* Portland: 1000 Friends of Oregon, 1993.

Alpha Engineering Inc., Walker Macy, Fletcher Farr Ayotte, and Iverson Associates. *Villebois: Specific Area Plan—South.* Vol. 5, *Rainwater Management Program.* Portland, OR: Alpha Engineering, Inc., 2003.

American Association of State Highway and Transportation Officials (AASHTO). *A Policy on Geometric Design of Highways and Streets.* No. 33. Washington, DC: AASHTO, 1994.

American Forests. *Regional Ecosystem Analysis for the Willamette/Lower Columbia Region of Northwestern Oregon and Southwestern Washington.* Washington, DC: American Forests, 2001.

————. *Regional Ecosystem Analysis Puget Sound Metropolitan Area.* Washington, DC: American Forests, 1998.

American Society of Civil Engineers, National Association of Home Builders, and Urban Land Institute. *Residential Streets.* Washington, DC: Urban Land Institute, 1990.

Apfelbaum, S. I., J. Eppich, T. Price, and M. Sands. "The Prairie Crossing Project: Attaining Water Quality and Stormwater Management Goals in a Conservation Development." 2001. Available at http://www.prairiecrossing.com/pc/site/press-links.html.

Appleyard, D. "Urban Trees, Urban Forests: What Do They Mean?" In *Urban Forestry Conference, 13–16 November 1978.* ESF Publication 80-003. Syracuse: State University of New York, College of Environmental Sciences and Forestry, 1980.

Arnold, H. F. *Trees in Urban Design.* New York: Van Nostrand Reinhold, 1993.

Atkins, C. "Traffic Calming." In *Transportation Planning Handbook,* ed. J. D. Edwards. Washington, DC: Institute of Transportation Engineers, 1999.

Barton, H., M. Grant, and R. Guise. *Shaping Neighbourhoods: A Guide for Health, Sustainability and Vitality.* London: Spon Press, 2003.

Beasley, L. "'Living First' in Downtown Vancouver." *Zoning News,* April 2000.

Beatley, T. *Green Urbanism: Learning from European Cities.* Washington, DC: Island Press, 2000.

Beer, A., T. Delshammar, and P. Schildwacht. "A Changing Understanding of the Role of Greenspace in High-density Housing: A European Perspective." *Built Environment* 29, no. 2 (2003): 132–43.

Ben-Joseph, E. *Livability and Safety of Suburban Street Patterns: A Comparative Study.* Working Paper 641. Berkeley: Berkeley Institute of Urban and Regional Development and University of California Institute of Transportation Studies, 1995.

Benedict, M. A., and E. T. McMahon. "Green Infrastructure: Smart Conservation for the 21st Century." *Renewable Resources Journal* (Autumn 2002): 12–17.

Benfield, F. K., M. Raimi, and D.D.T. Chen. *Once There Were Greenfields: How Urban Sprawl Is Undermining America's Environment, Economy, and Social Fabric.* New York: Natural Resources Defense Council, 1999.

Bohl, C. C. *Place Making: Developing Town Centers, Main Streets, and Urban Villages.* Washington, DC: Urban Land Institute, 2002.

Bradford, S., M. Herron, and K. Greet. "Hometowns: Three Case Studies." *Builder* 19, no. 8 (July 1996): 107–113.

Brand, R. "The End of the Runway: Converting a Former Airport into Neighborhoods Highlights the Conflicts That Come with 'Smart Growth.'" *Landscape Architecture* 92, no. 12 (2002): 44, 46–47, 88–91.

Brinckman, J. "The Endangered Species Listings: Species Act Now Covers NW Salmon, Steelhead." *Oregonian,* March 17, 1999, A1.

Bureau of Environmental Services 2000. *Clean River Plan.* Portland, OR: City of Portland, Bureau of Environmental Services.

Calthorpe, P. *The Next American Metropolis.* New York: Princeton Architectural Press, 1993.

———. "The Urban Network: A Radical Proposal: A Pitch for a New Kind of Transportation Network." *Planning* 68, no. 5 (2002): 10–15.

Carson, R. *Silent Spring.* New York: Fawcett Crest, 1962.

Center for Watershed Protection. *Better Site Design: A Handbook for Changing Development Rules in Your Community.* Ellicott City, MD: Center for Watershed Protection, 1998.

Cervero, R., and C. Radisch. *Travel Choices in Pedestrian Versus Automobile Oriented Neighborhoods.* Working Paper UCTC No. 281. Berkeley: University of California Transportation Center, 1995.

City of Denver. *Game Plan: Creating a Strategy for Our Future.* Denver, CO: Denver Parks and Recreation, City and County of Denver, 2003.

———. *Stapleton Water Quality Guidelines.* Denver, CO: City of Denver, 2000.

City of Minneapolis. *Minneapolis Near Northside: Master Plan.* Minneapolis: City of Minneapolis, 2000.

City of Surrey, UBC James Taylor Chair in Landscape and Livable Environments, Pacific Resources Centre, Ramsay Worden Architects Ltd., and Reid Crowther & Partners Ltd. *East Clayton Neighbourhood Concept Plan.* Surrey, British Columbia: City of Surrey, 2000.

City of Vancouver. *Draft ODP By-law for South East False Creek.* Vancouver, British Columbia: City of Vancouver, 2005.

———. "South East False Creek Policy Statement." Vancouver, British Columbia: City of Vancouver, 2004.

City of Wilsonville (Oregon). "Tree Preservation and Protection—Planning and Land Development Ordinance." Wilsonville, OR: City of Wilsonville, 2002.

Club of Rome. *The Limits of Growth: A Report for the Club of Rome's Project on the Predicament of Mankind.* New York: Universe Books, 1972.

Condon, P. *Sustainable Urban Landscapes: the Surrey Design Charrette.* Vancouver, BC: University of British Columbia, James Taylor, Chair in Land-scape and Livable Environments, 1996.

Congress for the New Urbanism. *Charter of the New Urbanism*. New York: McGraw-Hill, 2000.

Cook, E. A. "Landscape Structure Indices for Assessing Urban Ecological Networks." *Landscape and Urban Planning* 58 (2002): 269–80.

Corner, J. "Aqueous Agents: The (Re)-presentation of Water in the Land-scape Architecture of Hargreaves Associates." *Process Architecture* no. 128 (1996): 46–59.

Costa Pacific Homes. "Villebois to Feature Cutting Edge Rainwater Man-agement and 'Green' Development Practices." Press release, March 20, 2003. Available at http://www.costapacific.com/CP_press_frmset2.html.

Crane, R. *The Impacts of Urban Form on Travel: A Critical Review.* Cambridge, MA: Lincoln Institute of Land Policy, 1999.

De Chiara, J., J. Panero, and M. Zelnik. *Time-saver Standards for Housing and Residential Development.* New York: McGraw-Hill, 1995.

Design Center for American Urban Landscape and University of Minnesota. *Bassett Creek Wetland Park: Redevelopment in a Landscape of Wetland Soils.* Minneapolis, MN: University of Minnesota, 1996.

Dramstad, W. E., J. D. Olson, and R. T.T. Forman. *Landscape Ecology Principles in Landscape Architecture and Land-use Planning.* Washington, DC: Harvard University Graduate School of Design, American Society of Landscape Architects, and Island Press, 1996.

Dreiseitl, H., D. Grau, and K.H.C. Ludwig, eds. *Waterscapes: Planning, Building and Designing with Water.* Boston: Birkhauser, 2001.

Duany, A. and E. Plater-Zyberk. *Towns and Town: Making Principles.* New York: Rizzoli, 1991.

Dunham-Jones, E. "Seventy-Five Percent." *Harvard Design Magazine* (Fall 2000): 4–12.

Dwyer, J. F., E. G. McPherson, H. W. Schroeder, and R. A. Rowntree. "Assess-ing the Benefits and Costs of the Urban Forest." *Journal of Arboriculture* 18, no. 5 (1992): 227–34.

Dwyer, J. F., D. J. Nowak, M. H. Noble, and S. M. Sisinni. *Connecting People with Ecosystems in the 21st Century: An Assessment of Our Nation's Urban Forests.* Portland, OR: U.S. Department of Agriculture Forest Service, Pacific Northwest Research Station, 2000.

Ehrlich, P. R. *The Population Bomb.* New York: Ballantine Books, 1968.

Ellis, W. C. "The Spatial Structure of Streets." In *On Streets,* ed. S. Anderson. Cambridge, MA: MIT Press, 1986.

Erickson, D. "Can Open Space Shape Development? The Relationship of Smart Growth and Open Space Planning." Unpublished manuscript.

Ewing, R. H. *Best Development Practices: Doing the Right Thing and Making Money at the Same Time.* Chicago: American Planning Association, Plan-ners Press, 1996.

———. *Transportation and Land Use Innovations: When You Can't Pave Your Way out of Congestion.* Chicago: American Planning Association, Planners Press, 1997.

Farnsworth, C. B. "Re-imaging the Future." June 1, 1999. Available at
http://www.housingzone.com/topics/pb/green/pb99fa018.asp.

Ferguson, B. K. *Introduction to Stormwater: Concept, Purpose, Design.* New York:
Wiley, 1998.

———. *Stormwater Infiltration.* Boca Raton, FL: Lewis, 1994.

Fisher, B. "From the Water's Edge (San Francisco)." *Urban Land* 58, no. 1
(1999): 72–77.

Forman, R.T.T. "The Missing Catalyst: Design and Planning with Ecology
Roots." In *Ecology and Design: Frameworks for Learning,* ed. B. Johnson
and K. Hill. Washington, DC: Island Press, 2002.

Forman, R.T.T., and M. Godron. *Landscape Ecology.* New York: Wiley, 1986.

Francis, M. *Village Homes: A Community by Design.* Washington, DC: Island
Press, 2003.

Frank, L. D., P. O. Engelke, and T. L. Schmid. *Health and Community Design.*
Washington, DC: Island Press, 2003.

Frank, L. D. and G. Pivo. "Impacts of Mixed Use and Density on Utilization
of Three Modes of Travel: Single Occupant Vehicle, Transit, and Walking." *Transportation Research Record* 1466 (1994): 44–52.

Freeman, A. "Above the Cut: The Big Dig Selects Landscape Teams for Three
New Parks in Downtown Boston." *Landscape Architecture* 93, no. 3
(2003): 62–67.

Frey, Hildebrand. *Designing the City: Towards a More Sustainable Urban Form.*
New York: E &FN Spon, 1999.

Gangnes, D. A. "Seattle's Green Streets Ripe for Modernization." October 2,
2003. Available at http://www.djc.com/news/co/11149502.html.

Gause, J. A., A. Garvin, S. R. Kellenberg, and Urban Land Institute. *Great
Planned Communities.* Washington, DC: Urban Land Institute, 2002.

Gillette, J. B. "A River Runs through It." *Landscape Architecture* 88, no. 4
(1998): 74–81, 92–96.

Girling, C. L., and K. I. Helphand. *Yard, Street, Park: The Design of Suburban
Open Space.* New York: Wiley, 1994.

Girling, C. L., and K. I. Helphand. "Retrofitting Suburbia: Bellevue, Washington." *Landscape and Urban Planning* 36 (1997): 301–3.

Girling, C. L., and R. Kellett. "Comparing Stormwater Impacts and Costs on
Three Neighborhood Plan Types." *Landscape Journal* 21, no. 1/2 (2002):
100–109.

Girling, C. L., and S. Lamb. "Comparing Alternative Urban Forestry Scenarios for the Royal Avenue Specific Plan in Eugene, OR." Unpublished
manuscript, Community Forestry Assistance Grant Program of the Oregon Department of Forestry, Available at http://www.oregoncommuni-
tytrees.org.

Great Plains/Rocky Mountain Hazardous Substance Research Center.
"Phytoremediation." 2004. Available at
http://www.engg.ksu.edu/HSRC/phytorem/home.html.

Greater Vancouver Regional District. *Creating Greater Vancouver's Green Zone.*
Vancouver, British Columbia: Greater Vancouver Regional District,
1993.

————. *Livable Region Strategic Plan.* Vancouver, British Columbia: Greater Vancouver Regional District, 1995.

Grey, G. W., and F. J. Deneke. *Urban Forestry.* 2nd ed. Malabar, FL: Krieger, 1992.

Handy, S., R. G. Brown, and K. S. Butler. *Planning for Street Connectivity: Getting from Here to There.* Planning Advisory Service Report No. 515. Chicago: American Planning Association, 2003.

Handy, S. L. "Understanding the Link between Urban Form and Non-work Travel Behavior." *Journal of Planning Education and Research* 15, no. 3 (1996): 183–98.

Heckscher, A., and P. C. Robinson. *Open Spaces: The Life of American Cities.* New York: Harper & Row, 1977.

Hobbs, F., N. Stoops, and U.S. Bureau of the Census. *U.S. Bureau of the Census, Census 2000 Special Reports, Series CENSR-4: Demographic Trends in the 20th Century.* Washington, DC: U.S. Government Printing Office, 2002.

Holtzclaw, J. "Explaining Urban Density and Travel Impacts on Auto Use." State of California Energy Resources Conservation and Development Commission Docket No. 89-CR-90. Sacramento: State of California, 1991.

Hough, M. *Cities and Natural Process.* New York: Routledge, 1995.

————. *City Form and Natural Process: Towards a New Urban Vernacular.* London: Croom Helm, 1984.

————. "Looking beneath the Surface: Teaching a Landscape Ethic." In *Ecology and Design: Frameworks for Learning,* ed. B. Johnson and K. Hill. Washington, DC: Island Press, 2002.

Hu, P. S., and J. R. Young. *Summary of Travel Trends: 1995 Nationwide Personal Transportation Survey.* Washington, DC: U.S. Department of Transportation, Federal Highway Administration, 1999.

Hulse, D., S. Gregory, and J. Baker, eds. *Willamette River Basin Planning Atlas: Trajectories of Environmental and Ecological Change.* Corvallis: Oregon State University Press, 2002.

Institute of Transportation Engineers (ITE). *ITE Trip Generation Handbook.* Washington, DC: ITE, 1998.

Jack Faucett Associates and Sierra Research. "Background Information for Land Use SIP Policy." Washington, DC: U.S. Environmental Protection Agency, 1998.

Jacobs, A. B. *Great Streets.* Cambridge, MA: MIT Press, 1993.

Jacobs, J. *The Death and Life of Great American Cities.* New York: Modern Library, 1993.

JHK & Associates. *Accessibility Measures and Transportation Impact Factor Study.* Prepared for Transportation and Growth Management Program, Oregon Department of Land Conservation and Development and Oregon Department of Transportation. 1996.

Johnson, B., and K. Hill. *Ecology and Design: Frameworks for Learning.* Washington, DC: Island Press, 2002.

Johnson, C. "Fewer Vehicles on Road as People Opt for Transit." *Vancouver Sun,* August 30, 2004.

Johnson, S. A., and R. E. Lang. "Changing the Grid." *Urban Land* 59, no. 7 (2000): 48–53, 110–11.

Kalkbrenner, N. M., R. W. Wolfe, and J. F. New and Associates Inc. "Coffee Creek Center, an Ecological Restoration in Porter County, Indiana." Presented at the Wetlands 2002 National Symposium, October 7–9, 2002, Indianapolis, Indiana.

Kane, R. C. "Prairie Flower." *Landscape Architecture* 93, no. 10 (2003): 122–31, 156–59.

Kaplan, R. "The Green Experience." In *Humanscape: Environments for People,* ed. S. Kaplan and R. Kaplan. North Scituate, MA: Duxbury, 1978.

———. "The Nature of the View from Home: Psychological Benefits." *Environment and Behavior* 33, no. 4 (2001): 507–42.

Kaplan, R., and S. Kaplan. *The Experience of Nature: A Psychological Perspective.* Cambridge, MA: Cambridge University Press, 1989.

Kaplan, S. "The Restorative Environment: Nature and Human Experience." In Relf, D., Ed. *The Role of Horticulture in Human Well-being and Social Development: A National Symposium, 19–21 April 1990, Arlington, Virginia,* ed. D. Relf. Portland, OR: Timber, 1992.

Katz, B., and R. E. Lang, eds. *Redefining Urban and Suburban America.* Washington, DC: Brookings Institution Press, 2003.

Katz, P. *The New Urbanism: Toward an Architecture of Community.* New York: McGraw-Hill, 1994.

Kellett, R. *Measuring Infrastructure in New Community Development.* Eugene: Transportation and Growth Management Program of the Oregon Departments of Transportation, Land Conservation, and Development, 1999.

Kessler, J., and W. Schroeer. *Meeting Mobility and Air Quality Goals: Strategies That Work.* Washington, DC: U.S. Environmental Protection Agency, Office of Policy Analysis, 1993.

Landis, B. W., V. R. Vattikuti, R. M. Ottenburg, D. S. McLeod, and M. Guttenplan. *Modeling the Roadside Environment: A Pedestrian Level of Service.* TRB Paper No. 01-050. Tallahassee: Florida Department of Transportation, 2001.

Lecesse, M. "A Point Well Taken: Danadjieva & Koenig's "Stealth" Landscape for a Sewage Treatment Plant Matures on the Tip of Seattle's Discovery Park." *Landscape Architecture* 89, no. 6 (1999): 62–69.

———. "Dances with Water: Bill Wenk Strives to Unite Ecology and Infrastructure in the Colorado Prairie." *Landscape Architecture* 89, no. 2 (1999): 126–27.

———. "Plumbing the Heights." *Landscape Architecture* 85, no. 6 (1995): 54–57.

Little, C. E. *Greenways for America.* Baltimore, MD: Johns Hopkins University Press, 1990.

Loizeaux-Bennett, S. "Stormwater and Nonpoint-source Runoff: A Primer on Stormwater Management." *Erosion Control* 6, no. 7 (1999): 56–69.

Lund, H. "Testing the Claims of New Urbanism Local Access, Pedestrian Travel and Neighboring Behaviors." *APA Journal* 69, no. 4 (2003): 414–29.

Lynch, K. *A Theory of Good City Form.* Cambridge, MA: MIT Press, 1981.

Lynch, K., and G. Hack. *Site Planning.* Cambridge, MA: MIT Press, 1984.

Marcus, C. C., and W. Sarkissian. *Housing as if People Mattered: Site Design Guidelines for Medium-density Family Housing.* Berkeley: University of California Press, 1986.

McHarg, I. L. *Design with Nature.* Garden City, NY: Natural History Press, for the American Museum of Natural History, 1969.

McPherson, E. G. "Atmospheric Carbon Dioxide Reduction by Sacramento's Urban Forest." *Journal of Arboriculture* 24, no. 4 (1998): 215–23.

Metro. "2040 Growth Concept." 2004. Available at http://www.metro-region.org/article.cfm?ArticleID=231.

———. *Metro's Open Spaces Land Acquisition Report to Citizens.* Portland, OR: Metro, 2001.

———. "The Nature of 2040: The Region's 50-year Plan for Managing Growth." June 1, 2000. Available at http://www.metro-region.org/library_docs/land_use/2040history.pdf.

———. "Title 3 Model Ordinance." Portland, OR: Metro, 1998.

———. *Green Streets: Innovative Solutions for Stormwater and Stream Crossings.* Portland, OR: Metro, 2002.

———. *Trees for Green Streets: An Illustrated Guide.* Portland, OR: Metro, 2002.

Moll, G., and S. Ebenreck, eds. *Shading Our Cities: A Resource Guide for Urban and Community Forests.* Washington, DC: Island Press, 1989.

Morrish, William R. *Summary Report: Reclamation of Recreational Systems and Enviormental Resources from Existing Urban/Suburban Neighborhoods.* Minneapolis: Design Center for the American Urban Landscape, University of Minnesota, June 1993.

Moudon, A. V. *Effects of Site Design on Pedestrian Travel in Mixed-use, Medium-density Environments.* Olympia: Washington State Department of Transportation, 1997.

———. "The Evolution of Common Twentieth Century Residential Forms: An American Case Study." In *International Perspectives on the Urban Landscapes.* London: Routledge, 1991.

Moughtin, C. *Urban Design: Green Dimensions.* Oxford, England: Butterworth Architecture, 1996.

National Association of Home Builders (NAHB). *Housing Facts, Figures and Trends 2001.* Washington, DC: NAHB Public Affairs, 2001.

Neighborhoods Streets Project Stakeholders. *Neighborhood Street Design Guidelines.* Salem: Oregon Transportation and Growth Management Program, 2000.

Nelessen, A. C. *Visions for a New American Dream: Process, Principles, and an Ordinance to Plan and Design Small Communities.* Chicago: American Planning Association, Planners Press, 1994.

Neville, L. R. "Managing Urban Ecosystems: A Look to the Future of Urban Forestry." In *Handbook of Urban and Community Forestry in the Northeast,* ed. J. E. Kuser. New York: Kluwer Academic/Plenum, 2000.

Newman, O. *Community of Interest.* Garden City, NY: Anchor, 1980.

Northwest Environment Watch. *Cascadia Scorecard: Seven Key Trends Shaping the Northwest.* Seattle: Northwest Environment Watch, 2004.

———. "Fueling Up: Gasoline Consumption in the Pacific Northwest." 2002. Available at http://www.northwestwatch.org.

———. "Portland's 'Smart Growth' Pays Off, Clark County Comparison Shows." *Oregon Planners' Journal,* 2002. Available at http://www.northwestwatch.org/press/portland_sprawl.html.

———. "Sprawl and Smart Growth in Greater Seattle-Tacoma." 2002. Available at http://www.northwestwatch.org/press/seattle_sprawl.pdf.

———. "Sprawl and Smart Growth in Greater Vancouver: A Comparison of Vancouver, British Columbia with Seattle, Washington." 2002. Available at http://www.northwestwatch.org/press/recent_vansprawl.asp.

———. "Sprawl and Smart Growth in Metropolitan Portland: Comparing Portland, Oregon, with Vancouver, Washington during the 1990's." 2002. Available at http://www.northwestwatch.org/press/recent_portsprawl.asp.

———. *This Place on Earth 2002: Measuring What Matters.* Seattle: Northwest Environment Watch, 2002.

Noss, R. F. "Conservation of Biodiversity on Western Rangelands." In *Landscape Linkages and Biodiversity,* ed. W. E. Hudson. Washington, DC: Island Press, for Defenders of Wildlife, 1991.

Nowak, D. J., D. E. Crane, and J. F. Dwyer. "Compensatory Value of Urban Trees in the United States." *Journal of Arboriculture* 28, no. 4 (2002): 194–99.

Nowak, D. J., and J. F. Dwyer. "Understanding the Benefits and Costs of Urban Forest Ecosystems." In *Handbook of Urban and Community Forestry in the Northeast,* ed. J. E. Kuser. New York: Kluwer Academic/Plenum, 2000.

Noy, D. "Looking for Cycle-friendly Environments: Learning from Copenhagen, Denmark." Master's thesis, University of Oregon, 2001.

Olgyay, V. *Design with Climate: Bioclimatic Approach to Architectural Regionalism.* Princeton, NJ: Princeton University Press, 1963.

Peck, S. *Planning for Biodiversity: Issues and Examples.* Washington, DC: Island Press, 1998.

Perry, C. A. "The Neighborhood Unit." In *Regional Survey of New York and Its Environs,* 7 (1929): 34–44. New York: Regional Plan of New York and Its Environs.

Platt, R. H., R. A. Rowntree, and P. C. Muick, eds. *The Ecological City: Preserving and Restoring Urban Biodiversity.* Amherst: University of Massachusetts Press, 1994.

Podobnik, B. "The Social and Environmental Achievements of New Urbanism: Evidence from Orenco Station." Unpublished paper, Department of Sociology, Lewis and Clark College, 2002.

Poracsky, J., and M. C. Houck. "The Metropolitan Portland Urban Natural Resource Program." In *The Ecological City: Preserving and Restoring Urban Biodiversity,* eds. R. H. Platt, R. A. Rowntree, and P. C. Muick. Amherst: University of Massachusetts Press, 1994.

President's Commission on Americans Outdoors. *Americans Outdoors: The Legacy, the Challenge, with Case Studies: The Report of the President's Commission.* Washington, DC: Island Press, 1987.

President's Council on Sustainable Development. *Towards a Sustainable America: Advancing Prosperity, Opportunity, and a Healthy Environment for the 21st Century.* Washington, DC: President's Council on Sustainable Development, 1999.

Prince George's County (Maryland). *Low-impact Development: An Integrated Design Approach.* Largo, MD: Prince George's County, Department of Environmental Resources, 1999.

Punter, J. *The Vancouver Achievement: Urban Planning and Design.* Vancouver, British Columbia: University of British Columbia Press, 2003.

Read, N. "'More Bedrooms than People to Sleep in Them' in Richer Areas: Greater Vancouver's Growth Occurring Mostly in Its More Affordable Suburbs." *Vancouver Sun,* January 21, 2004.

Renner, M., and M. O. Sheehan. *Vital Signs 2003: The Trends That Are Shaping Our Future.* New York: Worldwatch Institute, 2003.

reSource Rethinking Building Inc., Harris Consulting Inc., Keen Engineering Co. Ltd., Hotson Bakker Architects, and Thornley BKG Consultants Inc. *Merge Consultancy Report for South East False Creek.* Vancouver, British Columbia: unpublished paper, 2003. Available at http:// Vancouver.ca/commsvs/southeast/documents/mergereport.pdf

Rinne, K. W. "Hydroscape/Cityscape." *Arcade* 19, no. 1 (2000): 23–25.

Rosenberg, E. "Public Works and Public Space: Rethinking the Urban Park." *Journal of Architectural Education* 50, no. 2 (1996): 89–103.

Sand Creek Regional Greenway. *Sand Creek Regional Greenway: Master Plan Report.* Denver, CO: Sand Creek Greenway.

Schueler, T. R., Center for Watershed Protection, and Metropolitan Washington Council of Governments. *Site Planning for Urban Stream Protection.* Washington, DC: Metropolitan Washington Council of Governments; Silver Spring, MD: Center for Watershed Protection, 1995.

Schuyler, D., J. T. Censer, C. F. Hoffman, and K. Hawkins, eds. *The Papers of Frederick Law Olmsted,* vol. 6, *The Years of Olmsted, Vaux & Company, 1865–1874.* Baltimore, MD: Johns Hopkins University Press, 1992.

Simpson, J. R., and E. G. McPherson. "Trees to Optimize Energy and CO_2 Benefits." In *Investing in Natural Capital: 2001 National Urban Forest Conference Proceedings, September 5–8, Washington, D.C.,* ed. C. Kollin. Washington, DC: American Forests, 2001.

Smart Growth Network. *Getting to Smart Growth II.* International City/County Management Association, 2003.

———. "Principles of Smart Growth." 2004. Available at http://www. smartgrowth.org/about/principles/.

Smith, D. S., and P. C. Hellmund. *Ecology of Greenways: Design and Function of Linear Conservation Areas.* Minneapolis: University of Minnesota Press, 1993.

Song, J., and G.-J. Knapp. "Measuring Urban Form: Is Portland Winning the War on Sprawl?" *Journal of the American Planning Association* 70, no. 2 (2004): 210–25.

Southworth, M. "Walkable Suburbs? An Evaluation of Neotraditional Communities at the Urban Edge." *Journal of the American Planning Association* 63, no. 1 (1997): 28–44.

Southworth, M., and E. Ben-Joseph. "Streets and the Shaping of Suburbia." *Journal of the American Planning Association* 61, no. 1 (1995): 65–81.

Southworth, M., and E. Ben-Joseph. *Streets and the Shaping of Towns and Cities.* New York: McGraw-Hill, 1997.

Spirn, A. W. "New Urbanism and the Environment." *Places* 13, no. 2 (2000): 44, 46.

———. *The Granite Garden: Urban Nature and Human Design.* New York: Basic Books, 1984.

Springgate, L., and R. Hoesterey. "Bellevue, Washington: Managing the Forest for Multiple Benefits." In *Urban Forest Landscapes: Integrating Multidisciplinary Perspectives,* ed. G. A. Bradley. Seattle: University of Washington Press, 1995.

Squires, G. D., ed. *Urban Sprawl: Causes, Consequences and Policy Responses.* Washington, DC: Urban Institute Press, 2002.

Stapleton Parks and Recreation Master Plan. Denver, CO: Park Creek Metropolitan District, 2002.

Stapleton Redevelopment Foundation. *Stapleton Development Plan.* Denver, CO: Forest City Development, 1999.

Statistics Canada. "Central Area Growth Statistics." 2003. City of Vancouver, http://vancouver. ca./commsvcs/cityplans/centralarea7.03.pdf.

———. "Kitsilano." 2003. City of Vancouver, http://www.city.vancouver.bc.ca.

Stein, C. S. *Toward New Towns for America.* New York: Reinhold, 1957.

Steuteville, R. "The New Urbanism: An Alternative to Modern, Automobile-oriented Planning and Development." *New Urban News,* July 8, 2004. Available at http://www.newurbannews.com/AboutNewUrbanism.html.

Steuteville, R. D. "New Neighborhoods Make Big Gains." *New Urban News* 9, no. 1 (2004): 1.

———, ed. *New Urbanism: Comprehensive Report and Best Practices Guide.* Ithaca, NY: New Urban Publications, 2001.

Stiffler, L., and R. McClure. "Our Troubled Sound: Spawning Coho Are Dying Early in Restored Creeks." *Seattle Post-Intelligencer,* February 6, 2003.

Strang, G. L. "Infrastructure as Landscape." *Places* 10, no. 3 (1996): 8–15.

Strom, S. "Urban and Community Forestry: Planning and Design." In *Handbook of Urban and Community Forestry in the Northeast,* ed. J. Kuser. New York: Kluwer Academic/Plenum, 2000.

Strutin, M. "Two Parks That Quiet the Storm." *Landscape Architecture* 81, no. 10 (1991): 84–87.

Swift, P. *Residential Street Typology and Injury Accident Frequency.* Longmont, CO: Swift and Associates, 1998.

Talen, E. "Pedestrian Access as a Measure of Urban Quality." *Planning Practice & Research* 17, no. 3 (2002): 257–78.

Tankel, Stanley B. "The Importance of Open Space in the Urban Pattern." In Wingo, Lowden Jr., *Cities and Space: The Future Use of Urban Land.* Baltimore: Johns Hopkins, 1963.

Thayer, R. L. "Increasingly Invisible Infrastructure." *Landscape Architecture* 85, no. 6 (1995): 136.

Tom Richman & Associates, Camp Dresser & McKee, and B. K. Ferguson. *Start at the Source: Residential Site Planning and Design Guidance Manual for Stormwater Quality Protection.* San Francisco: Bay Area Stormwater Management Association, 1997.

TreePeople. *Second Nature: Adapting LA's Landscape for Sustainable Living.* Beverly Hills, CA: TreePeople, 1999.

Tunney, K. W. "Innovative Stormwater Design: The Role of the Landscape Architect." *Stormwater* 2, no. 1 (2001): 30–34, 36, 38, 40, 42, 43.

Ulrich, R. S. "Benefits of Urban Greening for Human Well-being." In *Proceedings of the Urban Greening and Landscape Architecture Research Symposium, Copenhagen, June 23–25, 1999,* ed. T. B. Randrup. Hoersholm, Denmark: Danish Forest and Landscape Research Institute. Proceedings No. 2-1999.

———. "The Role of Trees in Human Well-being and Health." In *Proceedings of the Fourth Urban Forestry Conference, St. Louis, October 1989,* ed. P. D. Rodbell. Washington, DC: American Forestry Association, 1989.

U.S. Bureau of the Census. "Table B-1." In *State and Metropolitan Area Data Book 1997–98.* 5th ed. Washington, DC: U.S. Bureau of the Census, 1998.

U.S. Department of Agriculture (USDA) Forest Service. *An Ecosystem Approach to Urban and Community Forestry.* Washington, DC: USDA Forest Service, 1993.

U.S. Department of Transportation. *National Personal Transportation Survey.* Washington, DC: U.S. Department of Transportation, 1995.

U.S. Environmental Protection Agency. *Cooling Our Communities: A Guidebook on Tree Planting and Light Colored Surfacing.* Washington, DC: U.S. Environmental Protection Agency, 1992.

———. "Menu of B.M.P.s." 2004. Available at http://cfpub.epa.gov/npdes/stormwater.

———. "Non-point Source News Notes #44." Washington, DC: U.S. Environmental Protection Agency, Office of Water, 1996.

———. *Our Built and Natural Environments: A Technical Review of the Interactions between Land Use, Transportation, and Environmental Quality.* Washington, DC: U.S. Environmental Protection Agency, 2001.

U.S. Federal Housing Administration. *Planning Profitable Neighborhoods.* Technical Bulletin No. 7. Washington, DC: U.S. Federal Housing Administration, 1938.

Via Architecture, Hotson Baaker Boniface Hayden, StantecArchitecture, PWL Partnership Landscape Architects Ltd. *South East False Creek Official Development Plan–Urban Design Framework.* Vancouver, BC: City of Vancouver, unpublished paper, October 6, 2004.

Wackernagel, M., and W. Rees. *Our Ecological Footprint: Reducing Human Impact on the Earth.* Gabriola Island, British Columbia: New Society Publishers, 1996.

Walker Macy, Fletcher Farr Ayotte, Iverson Associates, Alpha Engineering

Inc., and William L. Owen & Associates. *Villebois: Specific Area Plan—South,* vol. 4, *Community Elements Plan.* Portland, OR: unpublished report, 2003.

Water Environment Federation and American Society of Civil Engineers. *Urban Runoff Quality Management.* Alexandria, VA: Water Environment Federation and American Society of Civil Engineers, 1998.

Wenk, W. E. "Toward an Inclusive Concept of Infrastructure." In *Ecology and Design: Frameworks for Learning,* eds. B. Johnson and K. Hill. Washington, DC: Island Press, 2002.

Wenk, W. E., and C. Gregg, "Stormwater Gardens (Convey, Capture, and Reuse: Stormwater)." *Landscape Journal,* Special Issue: Eco-Revelatory Design, 24–25.

Whyte, W. H. *The Last Landscape.* Garden City, NY: Doubleday, 1968.

Wolf, K. L. "From Tree to Forest." *Arcade* 21, no. 4 (2003).

Xiao, Q., E. G. McPherson, J. R. Simpson, and S. L. Usting. "Rainfall Interception by Sacramento's Urban Forest." *Journal of Arboriculture* 24, no. 4 (1998).

Index